BOOKS

THEIR CARE AND REPAIR

BOOKS

THEIR CARE AND REPAIR

JANE GREENFIELD

ADVISOR IN RARE BOOK CONSERVATION,
YALE UNIVERSITY LIBRARY

LECTURER IN BOOKBINDING,
YALE SCHOOL OF ART AND ARCHITECTURE

THE H. W. WILSON COMPANY

NEW YORK

1983

Library of Congress Cataloging in Publication Data

Greenfield, Jane.
    Books: their care and repair.

    Bibliography: p.
    Includes index.
    1. Books—Conservation and restoration.   I. Title.
Z701.G73   1984   025.7   83-25926
ISBN 0-8242-0695-9

Second Printing 1985
Third Printing 1992

Printed in the United States of America

CONTENTS

PREFACE vii

GLOSSARY 1
   Diagram, Parts of a book 11

GENERAL INFORMATION 12
   Book structure 12
   Causes of book deterioration 20
   Grain 22
   Determining grain direction 23
   Measuring 26
   Cutting 28
   Pasting 30
   Adhesives 31

THE SMALL BINDERY 34
   Necessary equipment 34
   Helpful but inessential equipment 38
   Small tools 42
   Expendable materials 49
   Suppliers 55
   List of suppliers by type of material 58

PAPER TREATMENT 60
   Treatments that can be done in-house 60
   Equipment and materials 61
   Dry cleaning 62
   Flattening 64
   Mending 67
   Pasting 72
   Storage 82
   Handling 82
   Encapsulation 83
   Bookplating 89

TIP-INS & POCKETS 91
   Equipment and materials 92
   Measuring 93
   Tipping in a single leaf 94
   Added stub 96
   Tipping in several single leaves 97
   Tipping in multiple leaves 98
   Tipping in a single folded sheet 101
   Tipping in several folded sheets 101
   Pages torn or cut out 103
   Pockets 104

PAMPHLET BINDING 108
   Equipment 110

Materials 111
Measuring 112
Single-signature pamphlet 113
Multiple-signature pamphlet 118
Adhesive-bound or side-stapled pamphlet 123
Unbindable material 126

HINGE & JOINT REPAIR 129
Attachment of bookblock to case 130
Equipment 131
Materials 133
Reinforcement of flyleaves 133
Broken hinges 134
Heavy bookblock 141
Flapping spine, boards still adhered 142
Hinges broken, joints broken or weak 151
Shaken hinges 154
Broken adhesive bindings 156

WRAPAROUNDS & KYLE WRAPPERS 159
Equipment and materials 159
Scoring and folding 160
Measuring 162
Wraparounds 163
Kyle wrappers 170

EXHIBITION TECHNIQUES 175
Environment 176
Equipment and materials 177
Holding books open 177
Supports and cradles 178
Books displayed upright 184
Books displayed slanting 185
Document mounts 188

BIBLIOGRAPHY 197

INDEX 201

PREFACE

This book is a basic manual for librarians, archivists, and all others who must personally face the problem of how to repair and care for books, pamphlets, documents, and other printed materials. Conservation of printed materials is a major responsibility for many people. Large libraries may have their own repair and conservation units, but most small and medium-sized libraries do not have this sort of facility, and so the task falls to the individual librarians, who must become competent and knowledgeable in this area.

In writing this book, I have made three assumptions about those I thought would most benefit from it: that they have not been trained in book repair; that they do not have unlimited funds; and that they would like to do as much as possible to improve and preserve the condition of the materials in their care. Therefore, Books: Their Care and Repair is not a book to be read through but one that should lie open on the workbench so that the detailed instructions can be followed step-by-step. Wherever possible I have used drawings to supplement the instructions and make them easier to follow.

Books: Their Care and Repair covers virtually all the basic repairs that one is likely to encounter: paper mending, tip-ins and pockets, the various types of pamphlet binding, hinge and joint repair, and protective covers (wraparounds and wrappers). In addition, it contains information on the basic structure of bound books, how to take care of them, causes of book deterioration, and the basic techniques of carrying out repairs -- measuring, cutting and pasting.

The book also includes a glossary of terms; a chapter called "The Small Bindery," which lists recommended equipment and expendable supplies; and a list of the names of some of the better known suppliers of materials called for by the instructions.

In 1980 very little had been written for small institutions about the treatment of so-called middle-of-the-road materials -- in between rare books and Harlequin romances. The subject of book repair and its importance to small libraries was almost completely ignored. At that time, I wrote a series of pamphlets on simple repairs that was published by the Yale University Library thanks to a National Endowment for the Humanities preservation grant. Books: Their Care and Repair grew out of this series, and the book updates and expands the original material. The audience for whom it is intended is still the librarian or archivist in a small institution.

I would like to thank the interns in the NEH program who tried out many of these techniques to see if my instructions were clear and if they worked; Shirley Prown, Conservation Studio, Yale University Library, and Sharon Pugsley, University of California, Irvine, for reading my manuscript for clarity; Carolyn Horton and Hedi Kyle for allowing me to include descriptions of their techniques; Wayne Eley for designing the bench described in "The Small Bindery", and Gisela Noack, Conservation Studio, Yale University Library, who used the pamphlets in workshops for Connecticut librarians and was able to suggest improvements in techniques based on the performance of the participants.

Kent Island
Squam Lake, N.H.

August 31, 1983

BOOKS: THEIR CARE AND REPAIR

GLOSSARY

In writing this glossary I have relied heavily on the book by Matt T. Roberts and Don Etherington, <u>Bookbinding and the Conservation of Books</u>, <u>A Dictionary of Descriptive Terminology</u>.

* *

ACID MIGRATION
Transfer of acid (highly damaging to paper) from one material to another by direct contact or by vapor transfer.

ADHESIVE BINDING
Single leaves held together by an adhesive (usually a PVA) rather than any form of sewing or mechanical attachment.

BACKING
Fanning out the binding edge of signatures to distribute the swelling caused by sewing and provide a groove into which the boards of the case can fit.

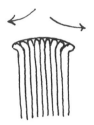

BED
The base of a press.

BINDING
Folded sheets or single leaves attached at one edge and protected by a cover.

BINDING EDGE
The edge of a bookblock that is held together by sewing or adhesion.

BOARD
A stiff, comparatively thick paper product used in making cases and other protective covers.

BOARD SHEARS
A heavy-duty cutter in which neither stationary nor shearing blade is very sharp but cutting is achieved by a scissor.

BOOKBLOCK
The textblock and any additions, such as endsheets that are added by the binder.

Reinforced endsheet *Book block*

BOOKCLOTH
A stiffened cloth made specifically for bookbinding.

BOOKWORMS
The larvae of a large number of beetles. They burrow into paper, causing considerable damage. The adults burrow out through bindings in order to mate.

BRISTOL BOARD
A very lightweight board.

BT
Board thickness. A measuring unit used in binding.

CASE
A protective cover made separately and then attached to the book, as opposed to a binding where the boards are laced to the bookblock before covering.

CASING IN
Attaching a case to a bookblock.

CHAIN LINES
Lines about 1" apart caused by supporting wires woven around the more closely spaced laid wires of a paper mold. They are parallel to the short side of handmade paper. Fake chain and laid lines can be impressed on machine-made papers.

CHAIN STITCH
A stitch that catches up previous sewing threads but is not sewn to a cord or tape.

CODEX FORMAT

The book as we know it today, made up of leaves in sequential order attached together at one edge and protected by a cover. This format superceded the roll (right) in about the fourth century.

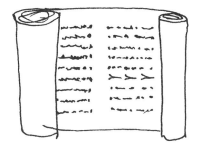

CONJUGATE LEAVES

Two leaves forming one piece of paper. Conjugate leaves are also called bifolios.

CORD

A string composed of several strands twisted together.

CORE

String or similar material on which a handmade headband is embroidered.

CRADLE

A structure, often of thin board, that supports a book on exhibition.

DAYLIGHT

The maximum possible space between the bed and platen of a press.

DURABILITY

The degree to which paper retains its original strength under heavy use.

ENCAPSULATION

Enclosure of a document between two sheets of polyester film by ultrasonic welding, sewing, or use of pressure-sensitive tape.

ENDSHEETS, ENDPAPERS

Blank or decorated papers at the front and back of a book. They can be blank leaves that are part of the first and last signatures of the textblock or they can be added by the binder. The case is glued to the outer ones in front and back. See PASTEDOWN.

FLYLEAVES
Endsheets except for any pasted to the inside of the board. See
also PASTEDOWN.

FOLIO
A sheet of paper folded once, forming two leaves, four pages. See
also CONJUGATE LEAVES.

FORE-EDGE
The edge of a book that opens. See diagram p. 11.

FORMAT
The general proportions and approximate size of a book. This origi-
nally depended on the number of times a sheet of paper was folded
(folio, one fold, quarto, two folds, etc.).

GATHERING
The process of collecting in order all the signatures that will make
up a complete book. See also SIGNATURE.

GRAIN
The direction in which the fibers of paper and paper materials fall
in the process of manufacture.

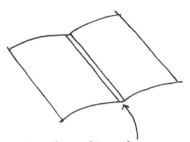

GUARD
A strip of material, usually paper,
used to join two leaves that are
apart but should be conjugate.

Guard attaching 2 leaves

GUTTER
The area inside a book that is adjacent to the binding edge.

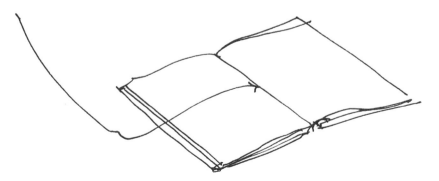

BOOKS: THEIR CARE AND REPAIR

HEAD
　　The top, particularly the top edge, of a book. See diagram p. 11.

HEADBAND
　　A strip of cloth tape embroidered at one edge, glued on the spine at head and tail and extending beyond the spine and onto the head and tail edges.

　　In the past and in hand binding, headbands were embroidered around a core and sewn into the folds in the signatures.

HINGE
　　The area between the spine edge of a board and the shoulder of a book. See diagram p. 11. Also a piece of paper attaching a document to a mount.

INLAY
　　A paper or thin Bristol board lining for the spine area of a case. See diagram p. 11.

JOINT
　　The area between a board and the shoulder of a book on the outside of the case. See diagram p. 11.

LABEL
　　A square or rectangular piece of material, usually paper, containing the title of a book and other pertinent information and pasted to the spine or the upper board of the case. See diagram p. 11.

LACED
　　The type of attachment of the bookblock to the binding in which the cords or tapes on which the bookblock is sewn pass in and out of the boards. At present this method is used only in hand binding.

LACUNA
　　A missing part, usually of a document or of a page in a book.

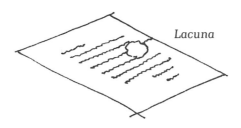

Lacuna

GLOSSARY

LEAF

A piece of paper consisting of two pages, one on each side. Leaves can be single or can result from the folding of a sheet to form a signature.

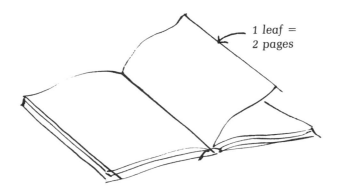

1 leaf = 2 pages

LEGS

The parts of a staple that go through the material being stapled.

MOISTURE BARRIER

A piece of paper, such as waxed paper, or polyester film, that prevents moisture from making adjacent paper wrinkle.

MULL

A lightweight, coarsely woven clothlike crinoline used to line the spine of books.

OCTAVO

A format made by folding a sheet of paper three times, making eight leaves, sixteen pages.

ORIENTAL SEWING

Sewing in which the thread goes through the bookblock at a right angle to it and also goes around the spine.

OVERSEWING

A mechanical sewing method in which small groups of leaves are sewn to each other by thread passing through them at a right angle to their plane.

PAGE

One side of a leaf.

PASTEDOWN
A piece of paper pasted to the inside of the board of the binding. It can be the first and last leaves of the endsheets or a separate leaf. See diagram p. 11.

PERMANENT
A term applied to paper that resists the effects of aging because of good quality materials and methods of manufacture.

PLATEN
The movable plate of a press that presses materials against the bed.

POCKET
A receptacle for loose materials. Pockets are usually made of thin board, such as Bristol board, and are attached to the inside of the lower board of the book.

POST
A double-headed screw, usually aluminum, used to hold single leaves together. Also the uprights of a press.

PRESS
A machine used to exert pressure or hold a book in a certain position while it is being worked on. The presses used in binding are called nipping or letter, lying, finishing and standing. See pp. 38-41.

PVA
Polyvinyl acetate emulsion, a very strong adhesive.

QUARTO
A format produced by folding a sheet of paper twice, making four leaves, eight pages.

REAM OF PAPER
Five hundred sheets.

RELATIVE HUMIDITY
"The ratio of the amount of water vapor in the air to the amount which would be present at the same temperature were the atmosphere to be fully saturated." (From Roberts and Etherington, Bookbinding and the Conservation of Books.)

REVERSIBLE
Capable of being undone. A requisite in conservation treatment of rare materials.

RING BINDER
A binder that holds leaves together by means of metal rings that can be opened or closed to add or remove leaves.

ROUNDING
  Shaping the sewn, glued spine of a book into a slight round. See
  also BACKING.

SCORE
  A slight indentation in paper or board made by running a blunt point
  along the line to be scored.

SCREW
  A ridged metal post that raises or lowers the platen of a press.

SHAKEN
  A term used to describe a book that is loose in its case but with
  the case intact.

SHEARING BLADE
  The moving arm of a board shears.

SHEET
  A full piece of paper.

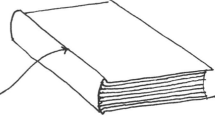

SHOULDER
  The part of the spine of a bookblock
  that is fanned out in backing.

SIDE SEWING
  Sewing that goes through the entire bookblock at a right angle to
  it. See also OVERSEWING.

SIGNATURE
  All the pages formed by the folding of a single sheet.

SPINE
  The bound edge of a book. See diagram p. 11.

SPINE LINING
  Cloth, such as lawn, muslin, super, or mull that lines the spine and
  extends about 1" on either side of it. Also paper glued on top of
  the cloth, the width of the spine only.

Cloth spine lining

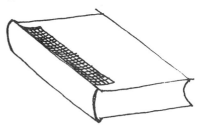

Paper spine lining

BOOKS: THEIR CARE AND REPAIR

SPIRAL BINDING
A binding of single leaves by means of a spiral-twisted wire or a plastic coil.

SQUARE
The portion of the board of a binding that extends beyond the bookblock.

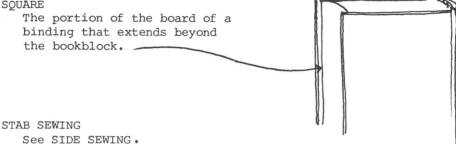

STAB SEWING
See SIDE SEWING.

STUB
An existing or added projection from a leaf that can be folded for sewing and to which an insert can be pasted.

Folded stub

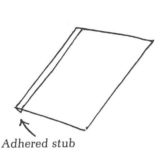

Adhered stub

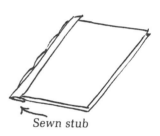

Sewn stub

SUPER
A coarsely woven fabric similar to lightweight crinoline used to line the spine of books.

SUPPORTS
Tapes or cords to which the signatures of a book are sewn.

TAIL
The bottom part, particularly the bottom edge, of a book. See diagram p. 11. See also HEAD.

TAPE
Linen or cotton tapes, from 1/4" to 3/4" wide, to which the signatures of a book may be sewn.

TEXTBLOCK
   The body of a book made up of leaves
   or signatures, excluding any papers
   added by the binder. See also
   BOOKBLOCK.

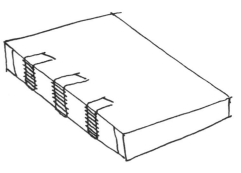

TIP-INS
   Any material such as replacements of missing parts or indexes that
   needs to be added in a book already bound.

TISSUE
   Very light paper used for mending.

TURN-IN
   The covering material turned in around the cover of a book. See
   diagram p. 11.

ULTRAVIOLET RADIATION
   Electromagnetic radiation of wavelengths shorter than visible light.
   It can cause fading and other damage to books and paper if they are
   exposed to it for long periods of time.

WARP
   The threads extended lengthwise in a loom.

WHIPSTITCHING
   The sewing of small groups of leaves over and over before sewing
   them on tapes.

WINDOW
   An area cut out of a piece of mat board, slightly smaller or larger
   than a document being displayed.

WRAPAROUND
   A protective cover made of thin board.

WRAPPER
   A protective cover made of a thin board, like Bristol board.

BOOKS: THEIR CARE AND REPAIR

PARTS OF A BOOK

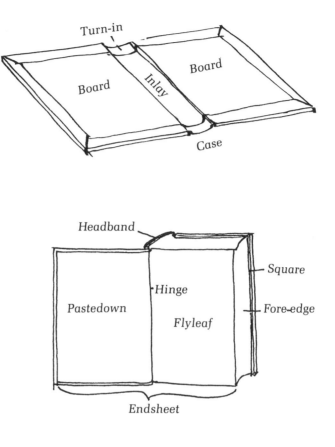

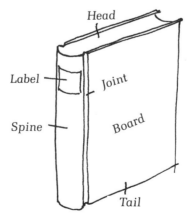

GENERAL INFORMATION

The book as we know it today, that is, the codex format, has been in use for about 2,000 years. Although there are endless variations in the way books can be bound, there are only two absolute requirements:

1. The order of the pages in the text must be preserved.

2. A protective cover must be added.

STRUCTURE OF A BOOK

The text of a book is made up of units based on the way the text is placed on pieces of paper and on whether, or how many times, that paper is folded.

Pieces of paper, not folded

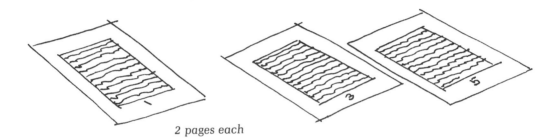

2 pages each

They can be put together -- bound -- in one of several ways:

Glue. Adhesive-bound books open easily right to the gutter margin and lie flat unless, as with paperbacks, a stiff cover is added.

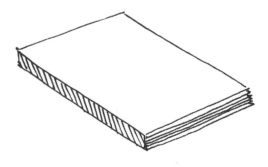

Sewing, stapling. Books can also be bound
by thread or metal that pierces the paper
at a right angle to its surface.

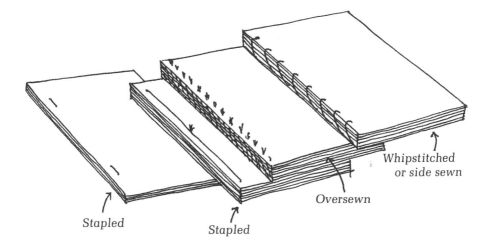

Stapled

Stapled

Oversewn

Whipstitched
or side sewn

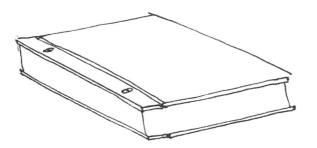

Aluminum post

All these books are
difficult to open.

Oriental binding is a form of stab
sewing, but Oriental books open well
because their paper is so flexible.

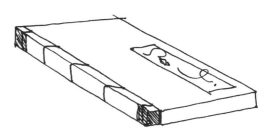

Ring and spiral binders are variations
on stab sewing, with the advantage
that they open all the way back to
the gutter edge.

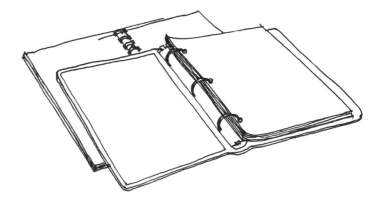

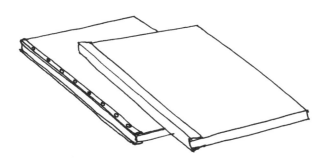

BOOKS: THEIR CARE AND REPAIR

Folded sheets

A sheet of paper can be printed on both sides and then folded one or many times. The folded sheet forms a unit called a signature, or gathering. The size of the book depends on the size of the original paper sheet and the number of folds.

In order to visualize the way a sheet is printed and folded to make up different formats, use pieces of typewriter paper to represent full sheets and fold them as follows:

Folio One fold

Number the pages, including the alternate numbers not shown in the drawing.

When you unfold the sheet you will see how it was printed.

1 sheet = 2 leaves = 4 pages.

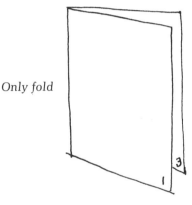

Only fold

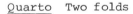

1 sheet

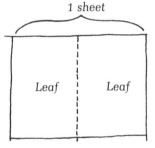

Leaf   *Leaf*

Quarto Two folds

Follow the same procedure.

1st fold

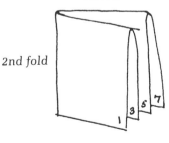

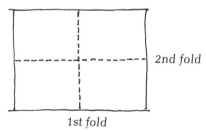

2nd fold   *2nd fold*

1st fold

1 sheet = 4 leaves = 8 pages.

<u>Octavo</u> Three folds

It is difficult to write the numbers
10 and 11 and 14 and 15 because they
are inside the first fold, but it
can be done.

The octavo is the most common format.

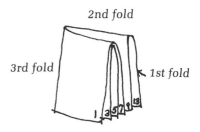

2nd fold

3rd fold

1st fold

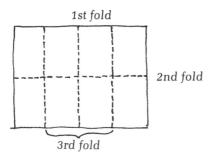

1st fold

2nd fold

3rd fold

Three folds = 8 leaves = 16 pages.

The choice of paper -- weight or stiffness in relation to the size
of the page, durability, and permanence -- is the most important
factor determining the quality of the book.

Folded signatures can be sewn to each other in one of two ways:

1. By a continuous thread running along
    the inside of the fold and coming
    out to form a chain stitch.

    In sewing, the needle is parallel
    to the plane of the paper.

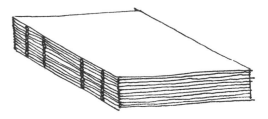

2. By a continuous thread coming out of the fold and passing around a cord or tape.

When the text of a book is adhered or sewn into a unit it is called a textblock.

The sewing threads inside the the folds cause a slight swelling at the spine.

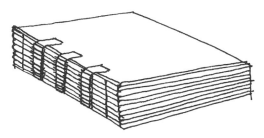

When the endsheet -- a folded sheet of blank paper, usually reinforced with cloth at the fold -- has been added, the textblock becomes a bookblock.

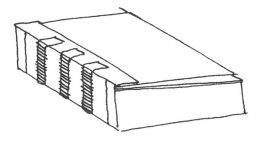

The spine is glued to help hold the signatures in alignment.

The book may be trimmed at this stage in the binding.

As you can see, the signatures still bulge at the spine.

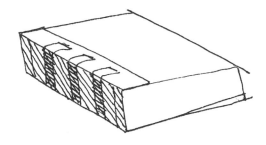

The book is then shaped:

The spine is rounded to reduce
the bulge caused by the sewing threads and to prevent
it from falling in like this.

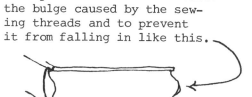

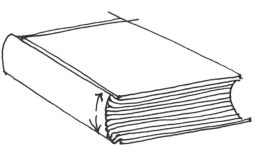

It is backed -- that is, the signatures
are fanned out -- to cut down further
on the bulge and provide a groove
for the boards of the cover.

The spine is lined with cloth, sometimes
with headbands at each end, and paper.

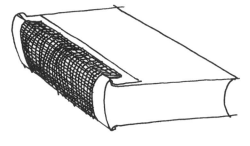

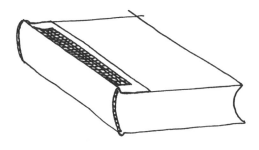

BOOKS: THEIR CARE AND REPAIR

In early bindings, and in some hand bindings today, the boards are laced onto the bookblock and then covered with leather or fine fabric.

This is a fifteenth-century binding with wooden boards, ready for covering.

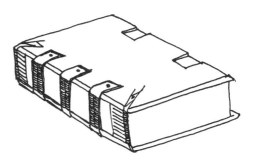

In most present-day bindings the cover boards and cloth are put together first and then adhered to the bookblock in a separate operation. This is called a case binding.

The case is made of two boards and a paper spine lining, or inlay, glued to an outer piece of cloth or other material. A narrow area of cloth is left without lining material at the joints.

The title is stamped on the spine of the case before the book is "cased in."

Casing in is the operation that attaches the bookblock to the case by adhesion. A properly fitting case supports the bookblock and vice versa.

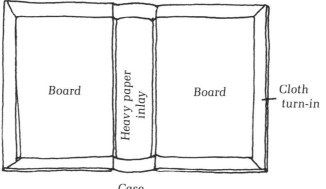

Board   *Heavy paper inlay*   *Board*   *Cloth turn-in*

Case

COMMON CAUSES OF BOOK DETERIORATION

The following is a brief summary of the subject. See pp. 197-199 for further reading.

Environment

Light: Causes fading and other chemical deterioration.

    Incandescent   ⎫ Least
    Fluorescent   ⎬ to
    Daylight   ⎬ most
    Direct sunlight   ⎭ damaging

Turn off lights when not in use.
Install ultraviolet sleeves on fluorescent light bulbs.
Install ultraviolet filters or curtains over windows and skylights.

Temperature: Heat makes printed and other materials brittle, and when books are stored in cold places condensation will form when they are moved to warmer temperatures.

The temperature range usually recommended is 68° - 74° F, but 65° - 68° is even better.

Keep books away from radiators.
Install air conditioning.
Ultraviolet filters are said to stabilize temperature and prevent rapid fluctuations.
Do not put incandescent lights in exhibition cases.

Humidity: A high humidity causes mold to form, a low one causes embrittlement.

Keep humidity below 70% and above 40% RH (relative humidity) if possible. Mold grown at 80° F and 70% RH in stagnant air, so keep air moving.

Install air conditioning or use dehumidifiers and fans in summer, humidifiers and/or pans of water in winter.

Air pollution: The filtration of sulphur dioxide, abrasive particles, and other pollutants will prolong the life of your books. However, this kind of climate control costs thousands of dollars to install and maintain and so is outside the scope of this book.

BOOKS: THEIR CARE AND REPAIR

Vermin

Cockroaches
Silverfish: Put a light coating of boric acid on the shelves <u>behind</u>
               <u>books</u> where children, or cats and dogs (should any come
               into your library), can't reach it. It is slightly
               toxic.

Bookworms: Freezing at 6° F for 12 hours should kill bookworms at
               any stage in their life cycle, including the eggs, but
               freezing for 72 hours at -20° F, although it may be
               overkill, is preferable. Books should be sealed in
               plastic bags before freezing to prevent moisture ex-
               change. Allow the condensation on the outside of the
               bags to evaporate before removing the books. This
               takes about 12 hours.

Rodents: Use commonly recommended methods of extermination.

Housekeeping

Dust, which is abrasive, settles mostly on the head of a book.
It can be removed with the soft brush attachment of a vacuum
cleaner or with a dust cloth.

When dusting, hold the book firmly closed with the head angled down
so that the dust is not forced down between the pages.

Shelves should also be cleaned periodically. Be sure they are completely dry before replacing the books.

An annual dusting and cleaning should suffice.

Handling

Shelve materials <u>upright</u> by size, not too tightly or loosely.
Shelve large books on their sides.

Remove the book from the shelf by grasping the middle of the spine.

Do not put anything in books: Papers
                                Paper clips
                                Flowers to press, etc.

Don't use rubber bands to hold a book together and <u>don't mend with</u>
<u>pressure-sensitive tape</u> unless the book is to be disposed of in the
forseeable future.

The materials used in books and in their repair have well-defined be-
havior patterns. These patterns and their effect on each other are
extremely important factors in the way a book functions and must always
be taken into account in book repair or binding.

GRAIN

The alignment of fibers in paper and board is called the grain. These
materials fold most easily parallel to the grain.

All the materials used in a book -- the paper of the bookblock, and the
board, cloth or paper of the binding -- should bend easily parallel to
the spine of the book or along the fold of a wraparound or wrapper.

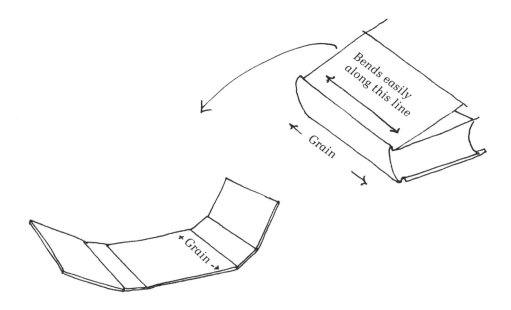

The extent to which material stretches is also related to the grain
direction.

Paper and cloth stretch and wrinkle more across than along the grain,
and this must be taken into consideration when using these materials.

BOOKS: THEIR CARE AND REPAIR

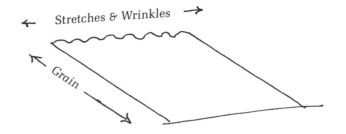

Stretches & Wrinkles

Grain

DETERMINING GRAIN DIRECTION

There are several ways of doing this:

Visually. Many papers, including most Japanese tissues, have lines, called chain lines, lighter than the rest of the paper and about 1" apart. These appear when the paper is held up to the light. The grain always runs parallel to these lines.

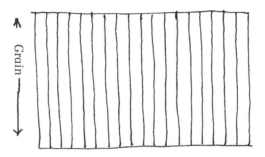

Grain

Tearing. If a paper does not have chain lines, its grain can be determined by tearing first in one direction and then in the other. The paper will tear easily and approximately in a straight line in the direction of the grain, but not across it.

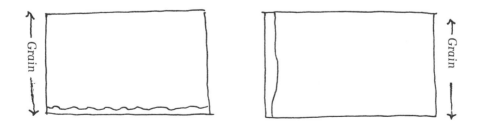

Grain   Grain

GENERAL INFORMATION

<u>Wetting.</u>

Wet two edges of a piece of paper.

One will wrinkle.
One will curl.

This drawing is
exaggerated.

The grain runs parallel to the curl.

<u>Bending.</u> This is a method that can be used for thin board, such as
Bristol board, as well as for paper.

Bend first in one direction, then in the other. Press down gently with
the palms of your hands. You will feel less resistance in one direction
than in the other. The direction of the least resistance is the direction
of the grain.

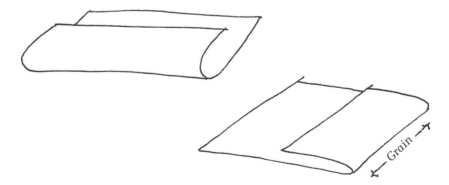

BOOKS: THEIR CARE AND REPAIR

You will soon find that you know the grain direction of the papers you usually work with when they are in large sheets, but not when they are cut up.

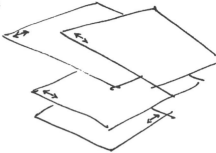

You will find that it saves time to mark the grain direction lightly in pencil on any useable scraps you save.

This is also true of board scraps.

The method used to determine the grain of board is different from that used for paper.

Put the board on a flat surface and bend one edge by placing your thumbs underneath and your fingers on top. Bend an edge at a right angle to the first in the same way. You will find that the board bends more easily in one direction than in the other. The grain is parallel to the direction in which the board bends and will fold more easily.

Notice the position of your hands:

In bending with the grain, the palm of your hands and your fingers rest on the board and curve with it.

In bending across the grain, your hands are forced to cup away from the board.

Cloth cannot be said to have a grain. However, it does fold more easily along the long warp threads, which run parallel to the length of the roll.

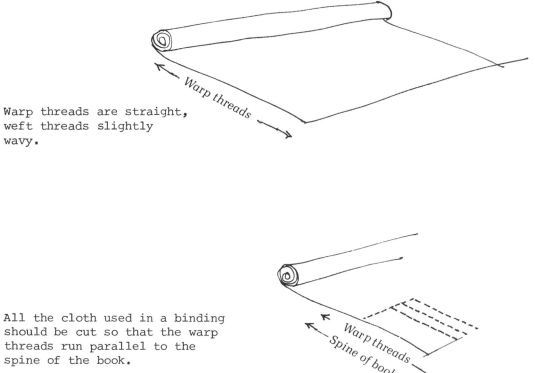

Warp threads are straight, weft threads slightly wavy.

All the cloth used in a binding should be cut so that the warp threads run parallel to the spine of the book.

MEASURING

The recording of dimensions in inches or centimeters interposes an unnecessary step in precise measurement and introduces error because measurements must be rounded off to the nearest subdivision of the measuring scale. It is also difficult to remember such measurements as 13 1/32" x 6 5/8" long enough to mark and cut or fold them.

In any case, it is impractical to measure a curved surface (such as a spine) with a ruler.

There are two easy ways to measure:

1. Mark the measurement on a strip of paper.

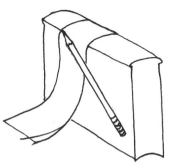

Width

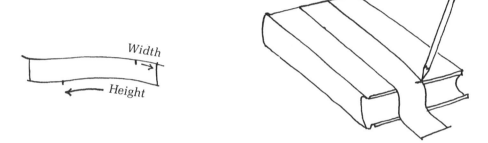
Width

Height

2. Put the material to be measured down on the material to be used and mark the measurement on the latter.

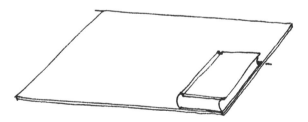

A dimension that is often used in measuring is a BT (board thickness). Naturally, it varies with the thickness of the board you are using.

Methods of measuring for each repair are described in the appropriate chapters.

If possible, use a cutter or board shears for cutting all types of material -- paper, cloth, or board.

If this is not possible, cut with a utility knife or scalpel along a straight edge.

Put the ruler down along the edge to be cut and press down firmly. Cut in the direction of the arrows, cutting away from you at the far edge so that the paper will not wrinkle at the beginning of the cut as it would if you pulled the blade toward you.

Cut on a piece of waste cardboard or thick binder's board. This will save the edge of the blade and the bench.

Cut lightly, using the edge as well as the point of the scalpel.

Several light cuts are better than one heavy one when cutting board.

Change the blade as soon as it becomes dull.

To cut a rectangular piece of material, make two marks equidistant from the edge.

BOOKS: THEIR CARE AND REPAIR

To make a parallel cut,
line up a straight edge
with the two marks.

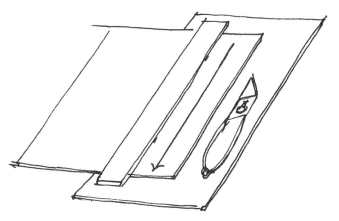

A sharp utility knife is best for
cutting board.

You need not cut away from you at
the far edge because board will
not wrinkle.

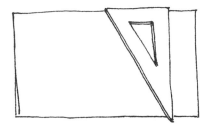

Cut the other two sides at a right
angle to your parallel cut.

A lot of cutting is needed in book
repair. Good quality scissors will
save you time and annoyance.

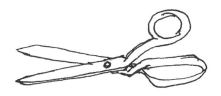

Pasting should always be done on waste sheets larger than the material to be pasted. When pasting, hold the material firmly in place so that it will not shift onto the pasted area of the waste sheet. Only your fingernails should touch the paper.

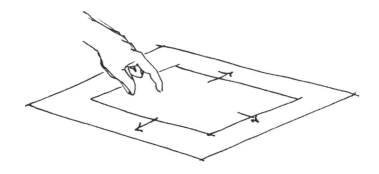

All waste sheets should be thrown away _immediately_ after pasting. It is very easy to put something you do _not_ want pasted, such as a book, down on a waste sheet that has wet adhesive on it.

Use waxed paper where it is needed to prevent moisture from penetrating adjacent materials or any excess adhesive from sticking where it is not wanted.

Always put a board and a weight on freshly pasted material and let it dry for several hours or overnight so that it will dry flat.

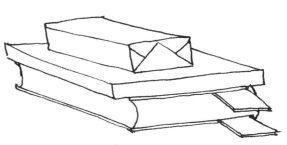

BOOKS: THEIR CARE AND REPAIR

ADHESIVES

PVA (polyvinyl acetate emulsion)

Although Elmer's Glue is a PVA, it is not recommended because it dries rigid.

PVA is very thick as it comes from the bottle and should be thinned slightly to make it easier to work with:

> 1/4 cup (59 ml) PVA
> 2 tbs. (30 ml) water

Wheat paste

Pastes are water soluble and so, easily reversible.

A very simple recipe:

> 1/4 cup (59 ml) water
> 3 1/4 level tsp. (6 grams) dry wheat paste
>
> Put the water in a container and add the
> wheat paste very gradually, stirring
> constantly until the paste is smooth.
> Let it set for several hours before using
> it. Store covered and refrigerated.

Cornstarch paste

An excellent paste can be made from cornstarch. It is so easy to make that a fresh supply can be made at frequent intervals.

> 2 to 2 1/2 level tsp. (6-7 grams) cornstarch, depending on
>   how thick you like your paste
> 1/2 cup (118 ml) water
>
> Dissolve the cornstarch in the water and cook, stirring
> constantly, directly over medium to high heat until it is
> translucent. This takes about one to three minutes.

The paste can be stored
covered with or without
refrigeration and will
last several days.
Stir if it separates.

If it goes bad (separates and has a bad smell), throw it away at once
and make a fresh supply.

Unless the use of PVA or paste (either wheat or cornstarch) is specified,
use the following mixture, which is a good, almost all-purpose, adhesive.

"50/50"

                1/2 PVA
                1/2 methyl cellulose

This recipe need not be followed exactly. Other proportions -- for
example 20 parts PVA to 80 parts methyl cellulose -- may work better
for you. It is worthwhile to experiment a little with slightly
different formulations.

Methyl cellulose, which is sold in granular form, must be mixed with
water before it is combined with the PVA.

                10 level tsp. (20 grams) methyl cellulose
                4 cups (946 ml) water

                Add the methyl cellulose to the water and mix well.
                Let it stand for several hours, stirring occasionally,
                before mixing with undiluted PVA.

Store mixed methyl cellulose in a covered container without refrigeration.

Adhesives may form mold in time and should be made up or decanted as
needed. Do not use any adhesive that has formed a mold.

PVA and 50/50 keep longer if stored in the refrigerator.

It is easy to glue a jar of PVA shut. To prevent this, keep the rim and
lid of the jar clean or put a piece of waxed paper or plastic over the
rim of the jar before screwing on the lid.

Care of brushes

When using an adhesive, fill the container
to a level slightly below the top of the
brush bristles. This prevents clogging
and helps to prolong the life of the brush.

PVA and 50/50 dry very quickly, so brushes
should be rinsed frequently. An alternative is to keep a glass of water and a rag
handy and to keep the brush in the water during
long pauses in pasting, drying it with the rag before resuming work.
Do not leave a brush in water for an extended period.

BOOKS: THEIR CARE AND REPAIR

After use, brushes should be washed in warm water far more thoroughly than seems necessary.

Excess water should be squeezed out with the fingers or a rag and the brush molded to its original shape, which it will retain when dry.

Sable watercolor brushes should only be used for paste that is water-soluble and easily washed out. After gentle washing in lukewarm water, shape the brush into a point while squeezing the water out.

Never leave a watercolor brush with the point down in water.

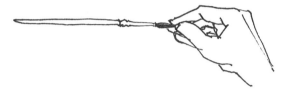

Stiff bristle brushes -- oil or house painting -- are best stored with their bristles hanging down so that residual adhesive doesn't build up at the base of the bristles along the metal ferrule.

It is easy to bore holes for strings in the wooden handles of oil painting brushes.

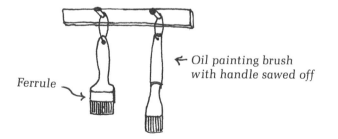

Ferrule ← ← *Oil painting brush with handle sawed off*

THE SMALL BINDERY

As always, having the right tool makes the job easier and more quickly
and efficiently done. All the optimum equipment needed to carry out the
repairs described in this book are discussed in this chapter, as is the
inexpensive equipment that can be substituted for it.

Only equipment and tools that are not in everyday use are described in
any detail with suppliers listed.

The equipment needed for each repair is listed at the beginning of the
chapter on that repair. Refer to this chapter for more detailed information.

NECESSARY EQUIPMENT

Binding or repair work should be done in a place set aside for that purpose, not in one already in use for another task.

Only five pieces of equipment are really necessary. They are, in order
of importance:

> Workbench or table
>
> Stool or chair
>
> Light
>
> Sink, or access to one
>
> Board shears or cutter

WORKBENCH

A sturdy table, as large as possible, will serve as a workbench.

Formica or polyurethane varnish provides a surface that is easy to keep
clean。

A workbench with useful storage areas underneath it can be made from
three 4' x 8' pieces of A-C plywood (smooth on one side), one 3/4"
the others 1/2" thick.

The plywood can be cut at the lumber yard as follows:

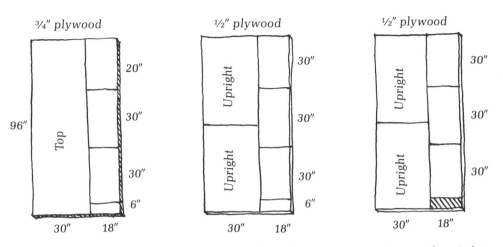

Tell the person who does the cutting that the measurements need not be full; in other words, the thickness of the saw blade may be deducted from them.

The height of the four uprights has not been specified as it depends on the height you like a bench to be. A bench high enough to allow you to work standing as well as sitting is useful. A height of 36"-37" is about right.

The 18" x 30" pieces are for shelves and the 6" x 18" pieces are used to box in 6" below the bottom shelves because shelves that rest on the floor collect dirt.

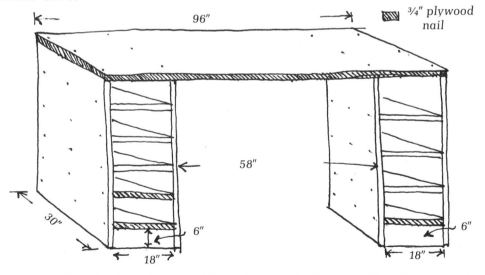

Construct the blocks of supporting shelves before nailing down the top.

STOOL OR CHAIR

A stool or chair should be 6" to 1 foot lower than the bench.
Stools are available in the following heights: 18", 24", 30".
They can also be cut down to the height you need.

LIGHT

If the light in your work room is not adequate it can be supple-
mented with a desk lamp such as this, which can be clamped to the
bench and turned in any direction.
Available from: Art supply and furniture stores.

SINK

A sink or access to one is necessary both because water is used for
some repairs and because brushes, adhesive containers, and hands need
frequent washing.

BOARD SHEARS OR CUTTERS

It is possible to cut board with a scalpel or utility knife and a
straight edge, but it is so difficult and time-consuming that board
shears or cutters are deemed to be necessary equipment.

Board shears

Board shears are large -- up to 4' x 10' -- and can weigh as much as
a ton. They are, however, the most efficient cutting machines available and well worth their high cost.
They are available in many sizes, sold by blade length. Board shears
with a 40" blade measure about 4' x 6'. A long blade allows

you to cut large pieces of board or cloth down to the size needed. Running a piece of beeswax along the edge of each shearing blade improves cutting.

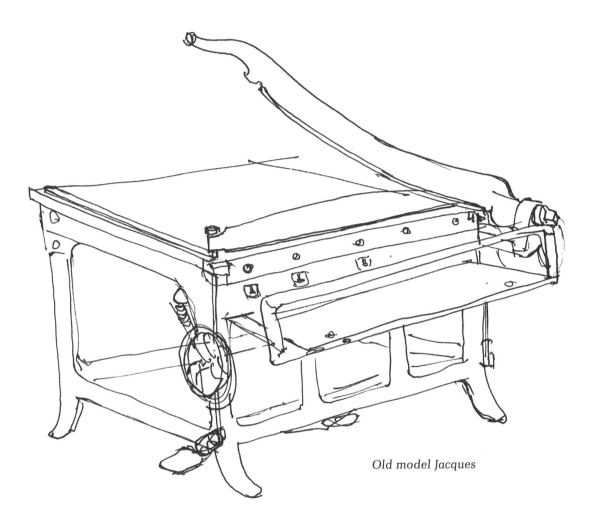

Old model Jacques

Available from: Gane Bros. (brand name Robust), Nixen Engineering (brand name Jacques), and occasionally from Schaefer (reconditioned) or from auctions or sales of printing or binding equipment.

Cutters

Lighter cutters with blade lengths ranging from 14-1/4" to 43-1/4" are available· All except the largest are table models.

Available from: BookMakers and Talas (brand name Kutrimmer), Gaylord and University Products (brand name Dahle)

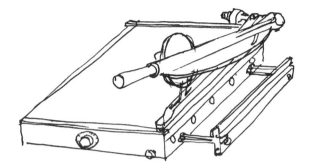

OTHER EQUIPMENT (OPTIONAL)

Helpful but inessential pieces of additional equipment include:

> Bookbinding presses
> Boards for pressing
> Humidifier
> Drill press
> Scoring machine
> Sewing machine
> Table for work that is drying or pressing

BOOKBINDING PRESSES

<u>Nipping or letter press</u>

   This type of press assures good adhesion when a book is being put back in its case.

   Heavy weights placed on a board or a book can take its place.

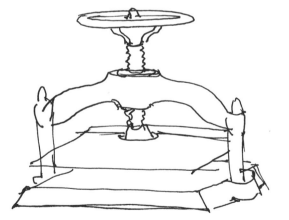

BOOKS: THEIR CARE AND REPAIR

Press sizes range from about 10" x 14", with 2" of daylight, to 16" x 24", with 36" of daylight. These presses are heavy and need a sturdy table to support them.

Available from: Antique shops, auctions or sales of binding or printing equipment, Gane Bros., Hickok, Schaefer, Talas.

Wooden lying press

This press holds a book with the spine up and rigid, so that it is easy to work on.

Sizes between screws range from 14" to 31".

Available from: BookMakers, Gane Bros., Hickok, Talas.

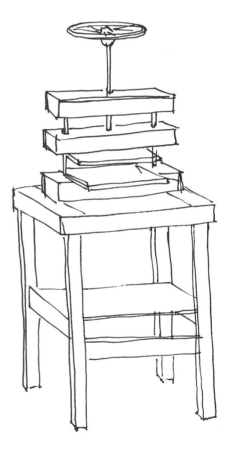

Cheeks

Combination press

This press performs all the functions already described in this section. It can also be used for other bookbinding functions which are not simple repairs but which are steps you will need to carry out if you become interested in bookbinding for its own sake.

The distance between posts when the press is used as a finishing or lying press is 20-1/2", and the platen, when it is used as a standing press, is 2" x 12" and opens 6". The stand is 20" x 28" by 30" high.

Available from: Harcourt, Hickok.

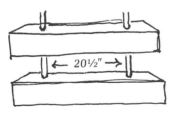

← 20½" →

THE SMALL BINDERY

A small combination press consisting of two boards held together with bolts and wing nuts also serves multiple functions, but is quite difficult to use.

It is 12" x 16".
Available from: Talas.

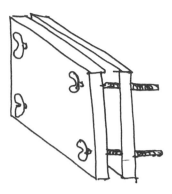

BOARDS FOR PRESSING

A wooden board should be put on either side of material that is to be pressed to protect the book from any roughness on the surfaces of the bed or platen of the press. If material is to be pressed under weights only, large books may be substituted for boards.

Pressing boards may be made of 1/2" A-A plywood (smooth on both sides), sanded and varnished. Polyurethane varnishes give a hard finish. A 4' x 8' piece of plywood can be cut at the lumber yard as follows:

9"	14"	14"	9"	29½"	29½"
12"					24"
12"			9"		
12"			9"		24"
12"			9"		

The measurements need not be full.

Keep pressing boards absolutely clean. Dirt will be transferred onto the material under pressure and a drop of hardened adhesive will make a dent in the material and the board itself.

BOOKS: THEIR CARE AND REPAIR

HUMIDIFIER

Any closed container large enough to hold a wet sponge in a saucer and the material to be humidified without their touching each other will serve as a humidifier.

A simple, effective one was invented by the conservator, Carolyn Horton.

It consists of a plastic waste basket inside a plastic trash barrel, with about 6" of water in the trash barrel. Empty the barrel and leave the top off when you are not humidifying.

Wash both waste basket and trash barrel occasionally with soap and water.

A sign on the cover of the trash barrel, reading "This is not trash. Do not empty." is advisable.

Available from: Sears, or hardware stores.

DRILL PRESS

This type of press is needed only if very large numbers of adhesive bound pamphlets are to be put into hard covers. Available from: Sears, or hardware stores.

SCORING MACHINE

Scoring a board so that it can be folded can be done with a bone folder and a straight edge. A groove, which can be made of three pieces of cardboard glued together, is helpful. See p. 171.

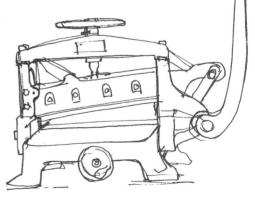

However, a hand operated guillotine with the blade dulled makes a far more satisfactory crease, and these are sometimes available for a reasonable sum. Large floor models are easier to find than small table models as there is less demand for them. They take up about 5' x 6' of floor space, the table model 41" x 44". A scoring machine called a case maker has been developed.

THE SMALL BINDERY

Available from: Auctions or sales of printing or binding equipment,
                  Hollinger (case maker), Schaefer.

SEWING MACHINE
   Sewn encapsulation envelopes are less expensive than, and
   preferable to, envelopes made with double-faced tape.
   A sewing machine is not necessary if, however, double-faced
   tape is being used. A domestic sewing machine is adequate
   unless a very large amount of material is to be encapsulated,
   in which case an industrial machine is needed.

TABLE
   An extra table for materials that are drying or flattening is very
   useful as it helps to keep the workbench clear for work.

                          SMALL TOOLS

ADHESIVE CONTAINERS
   Wide, shallow containers such as 1 lb. cottage cheese or refrigerator
   storage containers are best for adhesives because the brush will not
   make them tip over.

AWL
   A small awl is the most useful.
   Available from: Hardware stores.

BONE FOLDER
   Bone folders are available in various
   shapes and sizes, all useful. A pointed
   one is best for scoring and a slightly
   curved one for rubbing down.

   They should be kept clean but will
   discolor if left in water for any
   length of time.
   Available from: BookMakers, Harcourt, Talas.

BRUSHES

Cleaning

Any number of soft cleaning brushes
are available.

Japanese brushes:

Baby hair brushes, and soft
dust pan brushes:

Available from: Aiko's, Talas, drug or hardware stores.

Pasting

Fairly stiff brushes are best for pasting and will last for years
if properly cleaned and stored.

Useful sizes are:

2" cheap, stiff house painting brush

1" oil painting brush with the handle cut down so that the
brush is about 7-1/2" long and will not fall out of the
adhesive container. These brushes are comparatively expensive.

No. 6 watercolor brush, preferably of sable, which forms a
fine point. These brushes are also expensive.

Available from: Art supply and hardware stores.

COMBINATION SQUARE

Loosening the knob allows the
arm to move along the ruler.
Tightening it gives a
fixed measurement.

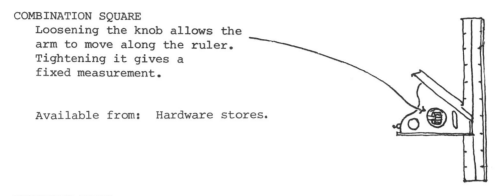

Available from: Hardware stores.

ELECTRIC DRILL

This is used to drill holes in adhesive-bound pamphlets. 1/16" and
1/8" drill bits are needed. A drill guide that enables you to drill
straight is available.

HOLEPUNCH

Holepunches that make oval or triangular
holes are best.

Available from: Some hardware or stationery stores.

KITCHEN KNIFE

A small paring knife can be used to remove staples. It should be
dulled and the point rounded so that it will not cut the paper.

MICROSPATULA

This is a very useful tool, particularly
for paper treatment.
Available from: Talas.

NEEDLES

No. 6 crewel needles, 4" mattress needles, No. 3 darning needles,
No. 11 sewing machine needles, and 14" No. 5
knitting needles.

PLASTIC BOTTLE WITH POINTED TOP (1 pt. Sobo bottle)

Used to coat a knitting needle with the right amount
of adhesive to repair a shaken binding.
Available from: Art supply and hardware stores.

PLATE GLASS

A piece of plate glass can be used as a pasting surface. The edges
should be sanded by the vendor and the glass handled with care as
even sanded edges can cut.

POLYESTER WEB
   This is a surprisingly durable material and one to which other
   materials will not stick. Hollytex No. 3221, 36" wide, is sold
   by the yard.
   Available from: Talas.

POTTER'S CUT-OFF NEEDLE
   Used to poke holes for sewing in thick signatures.
   Available from: Art supply stores.

SCALPEL
   A No. 4 handle with No. 23 blades is sturdy.
   Available from: BookMakers, Talas.

SCISSORS
   Stainless steel scissors, such
   as Fiscar, come in many shapes
   and keep their edge well.

   Available from: Cutlery, fabric, and hardware stores

STRAIGHT EDGE
   A heavy metal straight edge, although not a necessity, is better to
   cut against than an aluminum ruler. It is not possible to hold a
   flexible aluminum ruler down along its entire length and it is inclined to shift.
   Available from: Art supply stores, Talas.

TRIANGLE
   A 14", 40-60 plastic triangle is useful as the third
   angle is 45°.
   Available from: Art supply stores.

ULTRAVIOLET FILTERS
   Ultraviolet filtering sleeves for fluorescent lights are available
   from Solar Screen and Wei t'o. An ultraviolet filtering film which
   can be adhered to glass is available from Solar X of Connecticut.
   Also look under "Insulation Contractors -- Cold and Heat" in the
   yellow pages.

UTILITY KNIFE
   Better for heavy duty than a scalpel or X-acto.
   Use for cutting board. One with a retractable
   blade is best.
   Available from: Hardware stores.

WEIGHTS

Very heavy weights can be made by filling gallon plastic containers such as bleach or milk bottles with sand.

Bricks wrapped in paper or bookcloth also make good, fairly heavy weights of about 5 lbs.

Bricks can be covered with brown wrapping paper.

Fold a piece of paper tightly around the brick so that there is an overlap of about 1/2" and an extension slightly less than the thickness of the brick at each end.

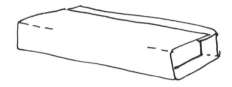

Remove the paper and crease each fold with a bone folder.

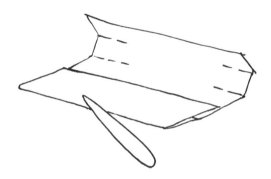

Glue about 1/2" along the edge and fold the paper back around the brick. Rub down the glued area with a bone folder.

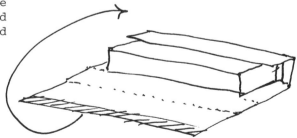

BOOKS: THEIR CARE AND REPAIR

Glue the shaded areas inside the
paper at the ends of the brick.

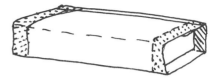

Fold down the top flaps.

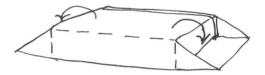

Glue the shaded area of the
side flaps.

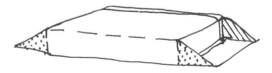

Fold them in.

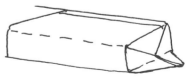

Glue the remaining triangles and
fold them up. Rub them down with
a bone folder and let them dry for
at least twenty minutes with a
weight against them.

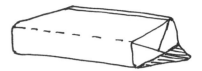

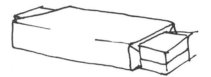

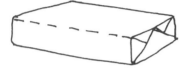

SMALL WEIGHTS

Rigid containers filled with heavy material such as pennies or shot
make good small weights (about 1 lb.).

A baby food jar is adequate for holding something
in position.

If you need to apply pressure as well as hold in position, use any
small container with a flat bottom. About 2-1/2" x 1-1/2" x 1/2" is
an ideal size since it need not get in the way of your hands as
larger weights are likely to do. Boxes with a ridge around the edge
(such as pin boxes) can be adhered to a piece of rigid binder's board
with double-faced tape.

BOOKS: THEIR CARE AND REPAIR

Although the list of small tools is long, all of them will fit in or around the workbench.

EXPENDABLE MATERIALS

The following supplies are those you will need to carry out all the repairs described in this book. Addresses for all suppliers mentioned can be found on pp. 56-57.

Storage

If possible store expendable materials in a dark, cool place because light and heat are bad for most of them.

Board and paper are best stored flat, and paper should be stored in a drawer or wrapped in a plastic garbage bag to prevent soiling.

If your storage space is limited, store board as upright as possible to prevent bending; store paper in a portfolio.

ACE BANDAGE
   Available from: Drug stores.

ACID-FREE PAPER
   More and more acid-free papers are being manufactured and used in publishing. The paper this book is printed on, for example, is acid-free. Paper merchants sell in large quantities (hundreds of sheets) only, but one acid-free paper called Permalife is available in small quantities from several suppliers. See also PERMALIFE PAPER.

APPLICATOR STICKS
   These wooden sticks are useful for applying small amounts of adhesive, as are toothpicks, or for making cotton swabs. Applicator sticks are available from scientific supply houses.

BARRIER BOARD
   Gray/white barrier board, .050 (a little less than 1/16" thick) is available in sheets 32" x 40" from the Hollinger Company.

BEESWAX
   Available from: Fabric or department stores.

BINDER'S BOARD
   This board is available in various sizes and thicknesses. Approximations of some of the thicknesses are:
      .060 = 1/16"
      .070 = a little more than 1/16"
      .088 = 3/32"
      .098 = a scant 1/8"
      .120 = 1/8"
   Available from: BookMakers, Gane Bros., Talas.

BLOTTING PAPER
   18" x 24", white.
   Facial tissues will serve the same purpose.
   Available from: Art supply and stationery stores.
BLUE WOOL SAMPLES
   They are small, 1-3/4" x 5-1/8", and are available from Talas in packages of 10.

BOOKCLOTH
   Two weights of cloth are needed for these repairs: Buckram, which is heavy, and Oxford, which is light. Both weights come in a 42" width and are sold by the yard.
   Available from: BookMakers, Holliston, Joanna Western, Talas.

BRISTOL BOARD
This is like a very thick paper. There are various ways of specifying thickness: .010, or 2-ply = about 1 index card in thickness; .020, or 3-ply = about 2 index cards. It is available from Talas and by the sheet or in pad form in various sizes from art supply stores. An acid-free Bristol called Permadur is available from Talas.

BUTTONS
Small metal buttons (about 1/2" across) with pins, No. 3613(149) gold, size 18, are available by the gross from the Blumenthal Company. They are also available in smaller quantities from fabric and department stores.

CARDBOARD
See WASTE MATERIALS.

CHARCOAL PAPER
A paper, usually of moderately good quality, available by the sheet or in pads from art supply stores.

CORD
Penn-Made linen cord is very strong. It is sold by the pound so it is cheaper to buy it unwaxed and wax it yourself. Six cord and 10 cord are useful sizes. Use 6 cord for small pamphlets, 10 cord for large ones. Available from: The Frederick J. Fawcett Co.

CORNSTARCH
One package will last a long time and is very inexpensive. Available from: Supermarkets, in 1-lb. packages.

COTTON SWABS
See APPLICATOR STICKS.

DEACIDIFICATION SOLUTION
Spray Wei t'o No. 11. Available from: Gaylord, Light Impressions, University Products, Wei t'o.

DOUBLE-FACED TAPE
3M No. 415, 1/4". It comes in 35-yd. rolls. Keep this tape wrapped in waxed paper when not in use as the sticky edges pick up dirt. Available from: Conservation Resources, Hollinger, Talas, University Products.

DUST CLOTHS
Treated dust cloths, such as "One Wipe" (Guardsman) and "Stretch 'n dust" (Chicopee), are lint-free and safe to use because they do not leave any harmful residues. Available from: Supermarkets or hardware stores or, by the dozen, from Talas.

GAMPI, THIN
   See JAPANESE TISSUES.

 GRAPH PAPER
    Available from: Art supply stores.

 GUM ERASERS
    Available from: Art supply stores.

JAPANESE TISSUES
   Strong, usually long-fibered papers. Those on the following list are
   good for mending.

      Gampi, thin, 20-1/4" x 32-1/4"
      Kizukishi, 28" x 36"
      Silk tissue, 18" x 24"
      Tenjugo, 21-1/2" x 31"
      Usumino, 23" x 35", #221-A (Aiko's)

   The availability of these tissues is somewhat uncertain, so give a
   supplier several alternatives when ordering.
   Available from: Aiko's, BookMakers, Panopticon, Talas.

KIZUKISHI
   See JAPANESE TISSUES.

 KNEADED ERASERS
    Available from: Art supply stores.

LAWN
   Available by the yard from fabric stores. It can be used to line
   the spines of small books.

LIG-FREE BOARD
   A good quality, light beige board that comes in two thicknesses:
   .020 (about 1/32") and .040 (a little less than 1/16"). It is
   available in sheets 32" x 40", grain short, or, if ordered in quan-
   tity, it can be cut to size.
   Available from: Conservation Resources.

 MAGIC RUB ERASER
    This eraser is said to be the safest to use.
    Available from: Art supply and stationery stores.

 MASKING TAPE
    Available in various widths from art supply and stationery stores.
    A width of 1/2" is useful.

MAT BOARD
Bainbridge manufactures acid-free mat board (32" x 40") in a wide variety of colors. Two-ply mat board is about 1/32" thick, four-ply is a little less than 1/16" thick.
Available from: Light Impressions and art supply and framing stores.

METHYL CELLULOSE
Available from: Talas.

MULL
A coarsely woven cloth for lining spines. See also SUPER.

MUSLIN
It can be used instead of super or mull to line spines and should be stronger because there are more threads to the inch. Available by the yard from fabric stores.

NEWSPRINT
A very poor quality paper which contains lignin and so carries the seeds of its own destruction. It is used only as a throwaway material. See also WASTE MATERIALS.
Available from: Art supply stores.

OPALINE PAD
Available from: Art supply stores.

PERMALIFE PAPER
A permanent, durable paper. The 20-lb. bond, 28" x 34", grain short, is similar to typewriter paper, the 70-lb. text, 23" x 35" or 25" x 38", grain long, is about twice the thickness of the bond.
Available from: BookMakers, Conservation Resources, Hollinger, Gaylord, Process Materials, Talas, University Products.

POLYESTER FILM
Mylar type D, .002 or .003 mil. This is available in rolls 20" or 40" x 100'. Single sheets and handling folders in standard sizes are also available. Melinex 0 or 516 is available in a choice of widths and thicknesses.
Available from: Gaylord, cut to standard sizes, I.C.I. America, Teitelbaum, Transilwrap, University Products.

PVA (polyvinyl acetate emulsion)
Available from: Art supply stores (brand name Sobo), Process Materials (brand name Promatco), Talas (brand name Elvace).

Q TIPS
Available from: Drug stores.

SANDPAPER
Fine, 150 sandpaper in 3-2/3" x 9" sheets is available in a package of six sheets from hardware stores.

SEINE TWINE
    No. 21 cotton, a strong string.
    Available from: Hardware stores。

SILK TISSUE
    See JAPANESE TISSUES.

STAPLES
    Staples made of rustproof Monel metal are available from Talas.

STORAGE CONTAINERS
    Archival storage containers are being made in ever-increasing numbers
    and sizes.
    Available from: Conservation Resources, Hollinger, Light Impressions,
    Process Materials, Talas, University Products。

STRATHMORE 400
    A moderately good quality paper that can be used for making document
    folders.
    Available from: Art supply stores in sizes up to 18" x 24".

SUPER
    A coarsely woven cloth for lining spines, similar to lightweight
    crinoline.
    Available from: BookMakers, Harcourt, Talas.
TENJUGO
    See JAPANESE TISSUES.

THREAD
    Barbour's linen 3 cord, No. 18 (heavy) and No. 30 (medium) come in
    50 gram spools and are available from Talas. Linen threads are also
    available from BookMakers and Harcourt。 Invisible nylon thread is
    available from fabric stores or department stores.

USUMINO
    See JAPANESE TISSUES.

WASTE MATERIALS
    Pasting sheets. These sheets are thrown away after one use. They
    can be made of inexpensive paper such as unprinted newsprint. Their
    size should be about 4" bigger than the material you are pasting, in
    both directions. Newsprint pads 12" x 18" or 18" x 24" are good
    sizes and are available from art supply stores.

    The ink from old newspapers will offprint onto light materials, but
    newspapers may be used for pasting dark cloth.

    Old telephone books are a source of small waste sheets because their
    ink does not offprint.

Waste board. Shirt cardboard or any other type of throwaway cardboard can be used as a cutting surface to save the surface of the workbench. A piece of masonite can also be used as a cutting surface, although it dulls the cutting blade more than cardboard.

Be sure the board is thick enough to prevent cutting through.

Waste paper strips. These strips, about 2" wide and longer than the material you are working on, are used to block off areas you do not want pasted. Their grain should be long so that adhesive will not seep under the wrinkles that would form if it were short. They can be cut from unprinted newsprint.

Waxed paper strips. They should also be about 2" wide and longer than the material you have pasted. Cut them parallel to the length of the roll as that is the grain direction of waxed paper.

WHEAT PASTE
   One half pound will last a long time. (See recipe, p. 31.)
   Available from: BookMakers and Talas.

WOODEN BLOCKS AND 2" x 4" PIECES OF LUMBER
   Unpainted blocks are the most unobtrusive.
   Available from: Toy shops, the 2" x 4"s from lumber yards.

LIST OF SUPPLIERS

The following short list contains the names and addresses of some of the principal suppliers to the book repairing community. Many materials may also be purchased at art supply stores, supermarkets, hardware stores, and department stores.

Those firms preceded by an asterisk sell expendable materials in small quantities.

On pp. 58-59 there is a list of the suppliers by type of material.

A comprehensive list of suppliers is available, to members only, from the Guild of Book Workers, 663 Fifth Avenue, New York, NY 10022. The Guild Newsletter often lists sales of secondhand binding equipment.

The Abbey Newsletter: Bookbinding and Conservation, c/o School of Library Service, 516 Butler Library, Columbia University, New York, NY 10027. This newsletter also lists sales of binding equipment.

*Aiko's Art Materials Import, Inc.
714 North Wabash Ave.
Chicago, IL 60611
(312)943-0745

B. Blumenthal & Co., Inc.
140 Kero Rd.
Carlstadt, NJ 07072
(201)935-6220

*BookMakers
2025 Eye St., N.W.
Washington, DC 20006
(202)296-6613

Conservation Resources International, Inc.
1111 North Royal St.
Alexandria, VA 22314
(703)549-6610

Frederick J. Fawcett, Inc.
129 South St.
Boston, MA 02111
(617)542-2370

Gane Brothers & Lane, Inc.
371 Route 17
Mahwah, NJ 07430
(201)529-1400

    1400 Greenleaf Ave.
    Elk Grove Village, IL 60007
    (312)593-3360

    1511 Mendel Dr., S.W.
    Atlanta, GA 30336
    (404)691-4050

    218 Littlefield Ave.
    South San Francisco, CA 94080
    (415)873-0850

    4697 E. 48th St.
    Vernon, CA 90058
    (213)582-8331

Gaylord Brothers, Inc.
P.O. Box 4901
Syracuse, NY 13221
(315)457-5070

    P.O. Box 8489
    Stockton, CA 95208
    (209)466-2576

*Harcourt Bindery
9-11 Harcourt St.
Boston, MA 02166
(617)536-5755

W. O. Hickok Mfg. Co.
P.O. Box 2433
Ninth and Cumberland Sts.
Harrisburg, PA 17105
(717)234-8041

The Hollinger Corp.
3810 S. Four Mile Run Dr.
Arlington, VA 22206
(703)671-6600

The Holliston Mills, Inc.
P.O. Box 940
Warehouse Rd.
Hyannis, MA 02601
(617)775-8409

I.C.I. America
Plastics Division
Wilmington, DE 19897
(302)575-3305

Joanna Western Mills Co.
151 W. 40th St.
New York, NY 10018
(212)695-5360

    P.O. Box 4299
    Long Beach, CA 90604
    (213)597-6565

BOOKS: THEIR CARE AND REPAIR

Joanna Western Mills Co.
2141 S. Jefferson St.
Chicago, IL 60616
(213)226-3232

    P.O. Box 19
    775 Washington St.
    Hanover, MA 02339
    (617)826-2119

Light Impressions
Box 3021
Rochester, NY 14614
(716)271-8960

Nixen Engineering Co., Inc.
P.O. Box 261
Mystic, CT 06355
(203)572-0241

Process Materials Corp.
301 Veterans Blvd.
Rutherford, NJ 07070
(201)935-2900

Ernest Schaefer, Inc.
731 Lehigh Ave.
Union, NJ 07083
(201)964-1280

Solar Screen, Inc.
53-11 105 St.
Corona, NY 11368
(212)592-8223

Solar-X of Connecticut
280 Boston Post Rd.
Orange, CT 06477
(202)865-8526

*Talas
213 West 35th St.
New York, NY 10001
(212)594-5791

*N. Teitelbaum Sons, Inc.
1575 Bronx River Ave.
Bronx, NY 10460
(212)892-3838

*Transilwrap Co. of New England
175 Tosca Dr.
Stoughton, MA 02072
(617)344-8535

*University Products, Inc.
P.O. Box 101 (South Canal St.)
Holyoke, MA 01040
(413)532-3372

*Wei t'o Associates, Inc.
P.O. Box 352
224 Early St.
Park Forest, IL 60466
(312)748-2995

LIST OF SUPPLIERS BY TYPE OF MATERIAL

Products in common use are not listed here.

Adhesives:
   Cornstarch: Supermarkets
   Methyl cellulose: Talas
   PVA: Art supply stores, Process Materials, Talas
   Wheat paste: BookMakers, Talas

Blue wool samples: Talas

Board:
   Barrier: Hollinger
   Binder's: BookMakers, Gane Bros., Talas
   Bristol: Art supply stores, Talas
   Lig-free: Conservation Resources
   Mat: Art supply and framing stores, Light Impressions

Board shears: Gane Bros., Nixen Engineering, Schaefer

Bone folders: BookMakers, Harcourt, Talas

Bookcloth: BookMakers, Holliston, Joanna Western, Talas

Brushes, Japanese: Aiko's, Talas

Buttons: Blumenthal, fabric stores

Combination square: Hardware stores

Cord: Fawcett

Cutters: BookMakers, Gaylord, Talas, University Products

Deacidification solution: Gaylord, Light Impressions, University
                      Products, Wei t'o

Double-faced tape: Conservation Resources, Hollinger, Talas, University
                    Products

Microspatula: Talas

Opaline pads: Art supply stores

Paper:
   Acid-free: BookMakers, Conservation Resources, Gaylord, Hollinger,
            Process Materials, Talas, University Products
   Graph: Art supply stores
   Japanese tissues: Aiko's, BookMakers, Talas
   Newsprint: Art supply stores

Polyester film:
   Melinex: I.C.I. America
   Mylar: Gaylord, Teitelbaum, Transilwrap, University Products

Polyester web: Talas

Potter's cut-off needle: Art supply stores

Presses:
   Combination: Harcourt, Hickok, Talas
   Lying: BookMakers, Gane Bros., Hickok, Talas
   Nipping or letter: Antique shops or sales of binding or printing
                     equipment, Gane Bros., Hickok, Schaefer, Talas

Scalpel: BookMakers, Talas

Scissors (rug shears): Talas, Westpfal

Scoring machine: Hollinger

Seine twine: Hardware stores

Staples, rustproof: Talas

Storage containers: Conservation Resources, Hollinger, Light Impres-
                     sions, Process Materials, Talas, University Products

Straight edge: Art supply stores, Talas

Super: BookMakers, Harcourt, Talas

Thread, linen: Bookbinder, BookMakers, Gane Bros., Harcourt

Ultraviolet filtering film: Solar X

Ultraviolet filtering sleeves: Solar Screen

PAPER TREATMENT

The techniques described in this chapter are suitable for the repair of research materials. The treatment of rare materials, however, should always be left to trained bookbinders or conservators. It is up to you, the librarian or curator, to evaluate your materials and to decide whether they should be cared for in-house by relatively inexperienced people or handed over to a trained expert.

None of the techniques described, if used carefully, will damage the materials and all are reversible.

Treatments that can be done in-house include:

> Cleaning
> Flattening
> Some mending
> Reproduction
> Provision of handling and storage containers
> Non-aqueous deacidification
> Encapsulation

Those that should be left to experts include:

> Aqueous deacidification
> Removal of pressure-sensitive tape
> Removal from acid mounts
> Stain removal
> Treatment of photographs
> Mending of **very fragile, brittle, or thin**
>   paper

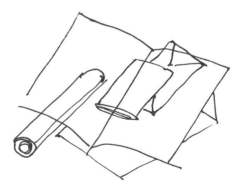

EQUIPMENT

Cutter or board shears
Pressing boards
Humidifier
Sewing machine
3 or 4 large weights
2 small weights
3 brushes for pasting
   2" house painting brush
   1" oil painting brush
   No. 6 watercolor brush
1 or 2 brushes for cleaning
Plate glass (optional)
Straight edge
Bone folder
Scissors
Scalpel
Sewing machine needles, No. 11
Microspatula
Eye-dropper
Adhesive container

MATERIALS

It is impossible to specify amounts to buy as many of these materials
can be used over and over. However, the amounts given in parentheses
are suitable amounts to buy for a start. Two or three sheets of
Japanese tissue, for example, are enough for several hundred mends.

Flattening:
   Newsprint (1 pad)
   Polyester web (5 yds.)

Dry cleaning:
   Opaline pads (2)
   Magic rub, kneaded and gum erasers (1 each)

Mending:
   Japanese tissue (2 or 3 sheets)
     Many thin, transparent (when adhered) Japanese tissues suitable
     for mending are available. Here is a partial list:
       Gampi, thin
       Kizukishi
       Silk tissue
       Tenjugo
       Usumino
   Newsprint

Wheat paste (1/2 lb.) or cornstarch paste (1 lb.)
Waxed paper (1 roll)
Blotting paper, white (1 sheet cut into 1" squares) or facial tissues
Cotton swabs or Q-tips (1 box)

Storage:
  Acid-free paper (50 sheets)
  An increasing number of storage containers -- file folders, boxes,
    envelopes, all of archival quality -- is becoming available.
    Amounts needed cannot be specified.

Handling supports and encapsulation:
  Deacidification solution (two 1 pt. spray cans)
  Thread, invisible nylon (3 spools)
  Staples (1 box)
  Polyester film (1 roll)
    Single sheets and handling folders in standard sizes are also
    available.

  Graph paper (2 or 3 sheets)
  Dust cloths (1 or 2)
  Double-faced tape (3 rolls)

DRY CLEANING

In some cases it is necessary to flatten paper (pp. 64-67) before dry
cleaning it, but if possible dry cleaning should be done first.

The various methods of cleaning are given in order of their abrasiveness,
starting with the least abrasive.

1. Brush loose surface dirt off
    with a soft brush, being par-
    ticularly careful if the
    paper is torn.

    Brush gently out toward the
    edges. Any motion in from an
    edge is likely to tear the
    paper.

    Very lightly sized and therefore
    fuzzy papers should only be
    lightly brushed without further
    cleaning.

BOOKS: THEIR CARE AND REPAIR

2. Use an Opaline pad for further cleaning. Squeeze some of the contents of the pad out through the knit outer cover and rub it gently over the surface of the paper with your fingers, using a circular movement in the center and moving out toward the edges.

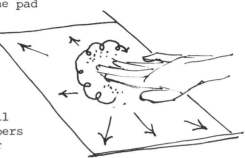

   Opaline pads will not remove pencil marks and are safe to use with papers other than the lightly sized paper mentioned above.

3. A slightly more abrasive, and therefore more effective, method is to squeeze out some of the contents of the pad and use the pad itself to rub the contents around on the paper.

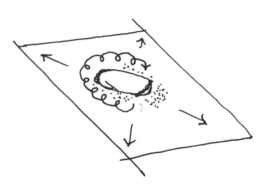

When you have finished cleaning, brush the crumbs from both sides of the paper and also from the work surface.

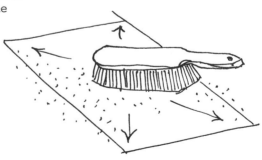

An eraser is more abrasive than an Opaline pad, but the Magic Rub eraser is said to do little or no damage if carefully used.

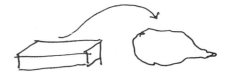

A kneaded eraser can be formed into any useful shape, such as a point, but should be used very lightly.

Do not erase on coated (shiny) paper.

An eraser can be used to lighten or remove very dirty spots.

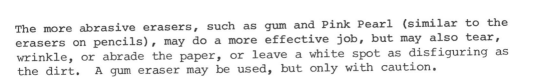

Erase the spot itself and then, more gently, erase outward from the spot so that the erasure is not sharply delineated.

The more abrasive erasers, such as gum and Pink Pearl (similar to the erasers on pencils), may do a more effective job, but may also tear, wrinkle, or abrade the paper, or leave a white spot as disfiguring as the dirt. A gum eraser may be used, but only with caution.

Dirt ingrained by frequent handling is impossible to erase and an attempt to do so can easily damage the document.

FLATTENING

A paper document that has been stored rolled or folded is disinclined to lie flat. Flattening is one of the first steps in treating it.

Humidifying relaxes paper; if it is allowed to dry under light pressure, it will usually stay flat.

BOOKS: THEIR CARE AND REPAIR

A simple humidifier is described on p. 41.

Place the material to be flattened on end in the waste basket. Leave it until it is limp and slightly damp.

Check periodically. The humidification process can take from half an hour to a day or two as different papers absorb water at different rates.

Heavy pressure, such as that exerted by a press, can change the character of a printed document or page. Fortunately, only light pressure is needed in flattening.

Make up a sandwich for pressing as follows:

   Cut 10 sheets of unprinted newsprint to the size of the boards to be used.

   Cut 2 pieces of polyester web to the same size. There are three reasons for using polyester:

   a) The document is protected from the highly acidic newsprint. (This may be over conservative.)

   b) It is easy to locate the document when taking the pressing sandwich apart. A document can be overlooked if its location in the sandwich is not marked in some way, particularly if more than one document is being pressed between the same boards.

   c) If there is any trace of damp adhesive on the document, it will not stick to the polyester web.

Both newsprint and polyester web can be used over and over again.

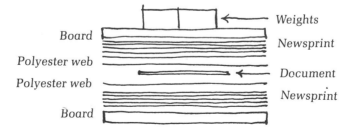

As many as three documents can be pressed at the same time. Each should be protected by polyester web and separated from the other documents in the sandwich by at least 5 sheets of newsprint. Three or four boards can also be piled one on top of another. This avoids the slight waviness caused by a large build up of paper.

In the case of multiple documents and/or boards, increase the number of weights.

Rolled documents

Have a board, 5 sheets of newsprint and 1 of polyester web ready to receive the damp document.

If the document has been stored rolled, put it on the polyester web with the inside of the roll down.

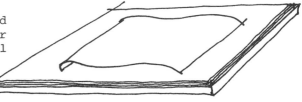

Press down gently on the humidified document, being sure that the curled edges are straightened out.

Put the other piece of polyester web and the other 5 sheets of newsprint on top of the document and smooth them down. Even their light weight will help to keep the document flat while you add the board and weights.

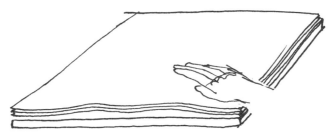

Let the document dry overnight.

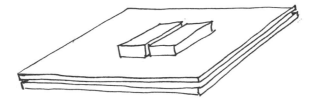

BOOKS: THEIR CARE AND REPAIR

Photographs on heavy paper, photostats, and blueprints often resist
flattening and need storage under pressure -- in a portfolio for example.

Folded documents

Many documents have areas along
a fold, or parts of their edges,
folded tightly over. In some
cases the text is obscured.

Put the document on the board,
newsprint, and polyester web and
turn the folded areas gently over
with a microspatula.

Press down on the crease with your
finger. The crease will probably
iron out because the document is
damp from the humidifier.

Add the polyester web, newsprint,
board, and weights and let the
document dry overnight.

MENDING

Only one type of mending is described here: traditional mending with
Japanese tissue and paste. This method is easily reversible in water
and can be used without taking a book apart.

Testing for ink solubility

Manuscript ink should be tested for water solubility before a wet mend is
made, as paste can cause the ink to run.

Put a drop of water on a period, comma, or other inconspicuous mark with
an eye-dropper. Let it soak in for a minute and blot it with a clean,
white piece of blotting paper or a facial tissue.

If a trace of ink shows on the blotter or tissue, do not mend the document.

How much to mend

As a general rule, mend only as much as is absolutely necessary.

    Book paper: The pages of a book need enough mending to be able to bend without further damage. Widely overlapping tears can be reinforced at the edge only; all others should be reinforced along their entire length. Corners need not be replaced but large lacunae should be filled in.

    Documents that are not to be encapsulated: They require the same amount of mending as does book paper as they are often subjected to the same stresses.

    Documents that are to be encapsulated: They require minimal mending as follows:

Small edge tears in documents to be encapsulated do not need mending, and long tears require only a small reinforcement at their edge.

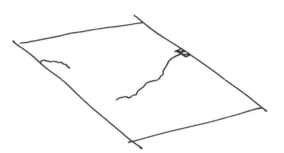

Lacunae in documents to be encapsulated require no mending.

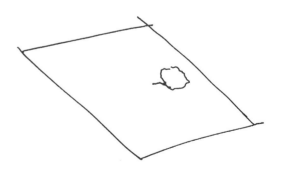

                                      BOOKS: THEIR CARE AND REPAIR

Separated parts of documents
should be reunited so that
they will not slide over each
other in the encapsulating
envelope.

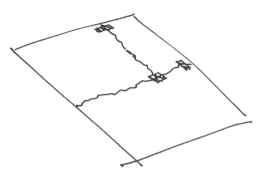

Supports for mending

When a tear lies within the bookblock,
the book can be propped open so that
the torn pages lie flat and supported
-- ready to be mended.

When a tear extends beyond the
bookblock, a level support must
be built up. This can be done
with pieces of cardboard or
binder's board.

PAPER TREATMENT

For a very thick support, substitute
a wooden board or another book for
several thicknesses of cardboard
and then add enough cardboard to
bring the support to the correct
level.

Add a thin piece of cardboard that supports the entire tear and a piece
of waxed paper before starting to mend.

Mending strips

When cutting Japanese tissue into mending strips,
make sure the grain of the paper runs with the
length of the strip.

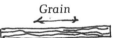

A mending strip cut or torn across the
grain will look like this when pasted
and will be difficult, if not impossible,
to handle.

Mending strips may be cut with a scalpel and a straight edge.

They should be about 1/2" wide.

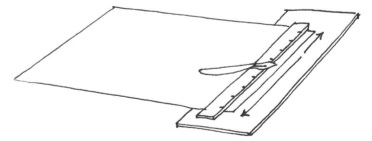

Torn mending strips and patches

If paper is fragile it may break along the edge of a reinforcement.
The long fibers of a torn strip provide a wide and tapering
reinforcement much less likely to do so.

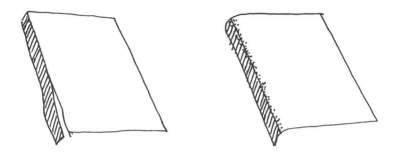

Mending strips may be torn by running
a wet cotton swab, such as a Q-tip,
along a straight edge. Remove the
straight edge and pull the strip
away from the sheet in the
direction of the arrows
so that the fibers are
splayed out.

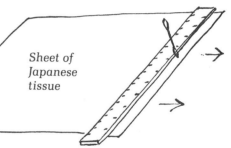

*Sheet of
Japanese
tissue*

Cut or tear mending strips only as needed, as they are difficult to store.

To tear patches for a lacuna,
put a piece of polyester film
over the lacuna to keep the
torn sheet from getting wet.

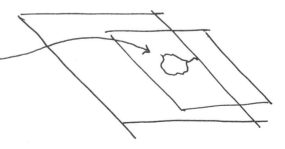

Put a piece of Japanese tissue
on top of the polyester film.

Draw around the lacuna with a
wet cotton swab. The patch
should be slightly larger
than the lacuna.

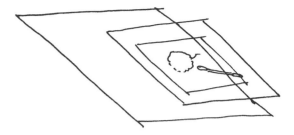

Tear the patch from the tissue.
It will tear easily where it is
wet.

Pull the surrounding tissue away
in the direction of the arrows.

Another patch, slightly larger
than the first, is needed for the
other side of the sheet.

The edges of reinforcements on both sides of a sheet should never line
up because fragile paper may break along a single reinforced edge.

PASTING

Mending strips may be pasted on a
waste sheet or strip of unprinted
newsprint.

Paste in the direction of the arrows,
being careful that the fibers of torn
strips stay splayed out.

Always throw waste sheets away
immediately after use.

If you are mending an edge tear, leave
an end of the strip unpasted so you can
pick it up.

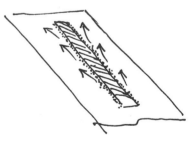

An alternate method of pasting is to lay the patch or strip down on a piece of glass to which you have already applied paste. This provides a thinner, more even coat of paste than pasting the tissue itself.

Paste an area on a piece of glass large enough to accommodate one or two mending strips. Use a 2" brush. Smooth the paste out without adding more.

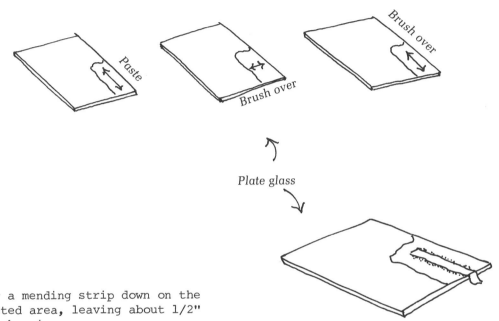

Plate glass

Lay a mending strip down on the pasted area, leaving about 1/2" overhanging.

Put a piece of waxed paper over the pasted area and rub down gently with your fingers.

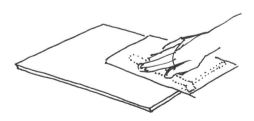

If the strip is not completely
transparent after it has been
rubbed down, but has white
streaks in it, it should be put
down again on a freshly pasted
area of glass. It will not be
necessary to rub it down.

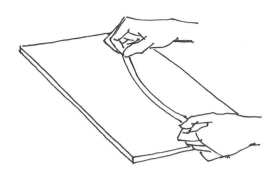

Overlapping tear

Paper often tears in such a way
that the edges of the tear
overlap. The overlapping
area is usually clearly
visible.

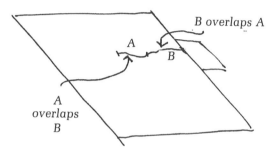

An overlapping tear frequently
changes direction. In repairing
such a tear, mend only one
direction at a time.

Put a piece of waxed paper
underneath the tear before
starting work so that any
excess paste will not cause
the sheet to stick to the
bench or one page to another.

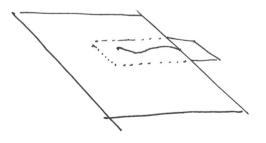

BOOKS: THEIR CARE AND REPAIR

Pasting the edges of a tear is best
done with a watercolor brush.

Lift A slightly and paste on top
of B.

Paste underneath A with the tip of
the brush.

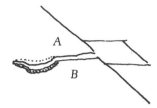

Alternatively bend A back,
being careful not to extend
the tear, and paste the two
edges.

Paste only to the point where the
overlap changes direction.

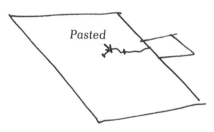

The edges of a tear are sometimes
slightly out of alignment.

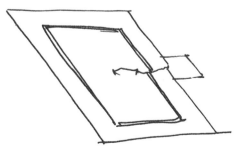

PAPER TREATMENT

Before putting A down on B, be
sure that the tear is aligned
along its entire length, including the unpasted part.

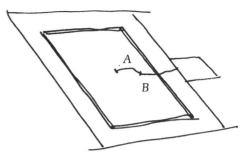

When the tear is correctly aligned,
put a piece of waxed paper on it
and rub down the pasted edges with
a bone folder.

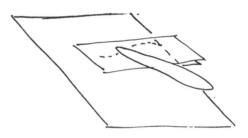

Leave the waxed paper in place
and put a small weight over the
mended part of the tear.

Let the mend dry for an hour or
more. It may not be completely
dry, but it will be dry enough to
be handled.

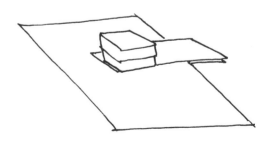

BOOKS: THEIR CARE AND REPAIR

Paste and put B down on A in the same way.

Let the mend dry overnight, under a board and a weight.

Occasionally tears do not change direction and may be mended in one operation.

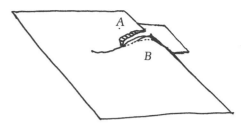

Reinforced mend

A tear with little or no overlap needs reinforcement.

Whenever possible, make an overlapping mend, however slight the overlap, and let it dry before adding a mending strip.

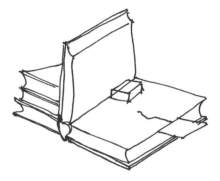

Put a piece of waxed paper under the tear.

If an overlapping mend was not made, align the edges of the tear and put a small weight on either side of it to hold the edges in position.

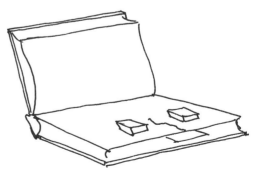

PAPER TREATMENT

Paste a mending strip slightly longer
than the tear.

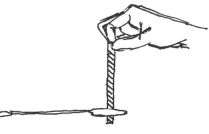

Pick up the strip by the unpasted
end, with the pasted side toward
you.

Put a microspatula against the
pasted side of the strip, at its
other end,

and lift the strip into a
horizontal position,
pasted side down.

Position the strip on the tear,
leaving the unpasted section
overhanging the edge.

Slide the microspatula out
from under the strip in the
direction of the arrow.

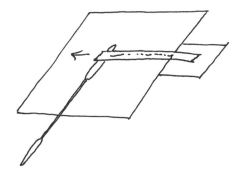

BOOKS: THEIR CARE AND REPAIR

Put a piece of waxed paper over the tear, close the book and let the mend dry overnight under a weight.

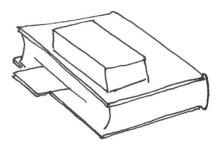

When the mend is dry, trim the mending strip flush at the edge of the page or leave about 1/8" extending, add paste, and fold it around to the other side of the page.

This necessitates, yet again, drying between pieces of waxed paper, under pressure.

A widely overlapping tear needs only a small edge reinforcement.

Paste about 1/2" of a short mending strip, position it (no microspatula is needed), let it dry, and trim it flush or turn it around as described above.

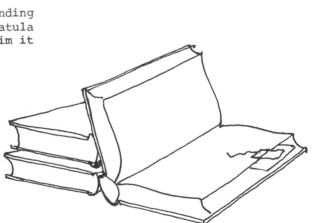

Filling in lacunae

Filling in a lacuna at the edge of
a sheet can be done in the way
described for reinforced tears --
that is, by leaving the extending
part of the mending tissue unpasted and so easy to handle.

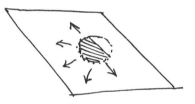

Apply a patch to each side of the
sheet and rub down and dry under
pressure as already described.

Trim off the extending tissue when
the mend is dry.

When a lacuna is in from the edge
of a sheet, the whole patch needs
to be pasted:

Paste the tissue except for a
part large enough to be picked up.

If the patch is large, paste
about 1/3 of it only. (Practice
in adhering large patches is
advisable.)

Be sure to paste the side of the
patch that goes <u>down</u> on the lacuna,
particularly if the lacuna is
irregular.

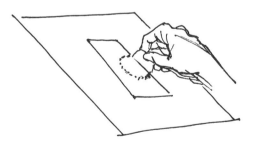

Position the pasted part of the
tissue on the lacuna and fold
the unpasted part back onto a
small piece of waxed paper.

BOOKS: THEIR CARE AND REPAIR

Paste the remainder of the tissue
in the direction of the arrows,
being careful to paste on the
waxed paper only and not on any
part of the document.

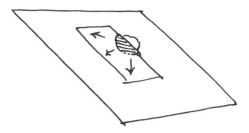

Fold the waxed paper over and slide
or roll it away from the pasted
tissue.

Do not fold it all the way down
onto the document as it has paste
on it.

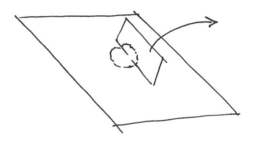

Throw the waxed paper away.

Smooth the patch down with your finger.

Add a piece of waxed paper, rub down
with a bone folder and let the mend
dry for half an hour before repeating
the process with a patch on the other
side.

Let the finished mend dry overnight
between pieces of waxed paper under
pressure.

PAPER TREATMENT   81

STORAGE

Acid migration, which can do serious damage, can be prevented by using archival quality storage containers -- file folders and storage boxes.

To prevent acid migration from paper to paper within an outer storage folder, an acid-free paper folder can be used. It will act as a barrier between valuable materials and auxiliary materials, which may be highly acidic.

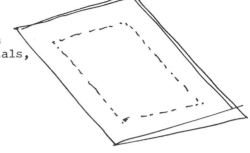

Sheets of acid-free paper a little more than twice the size of letter (12" x 18") or legal (15" x 18") size typewriter paper can be used to make such folders.

Alternatively, photocopy the necessary auxiliary material on archival quality paper and store the originals elsewhere.

HANDLING

Use is wearing on all materials. Copies of rare or fragile documents may satisfy readers' needs, but the original document can be seen if it is vital to research. Archival materials can be photocopied or micro-filmed, photocopying being considerably less expensive than microfilming.

The use of an archive can be extended by having a copy available in more than one research facility -- for example, in both a local museum and an historical society.

Handling supports

Documents can be put in polyester film supports before being handed to readers. This cuts down on mechanical wear.

The supports can be made of polyester film sheets sewn or taped together in-house and appropriate for the average size of the documents involved, or bought in the standard sizes increasingly available.

ENCAPSULATION

Encapsulation is not necessarily a permanent method of storage as the sealed or sewn edges of the envelope can easily be cut off, leaving the material in its original condition. Thus it is as reversible as any technique can well be.

However, encapsulation is more permanent than putting the material in a support while it is being handled.

If possible, all materials should be deacidified before they are encapsulated. Aqueous deacidification requires experience in handling wet paper, which is fragile and easily torn, but non-aqueous deacidification solutions are available.

Wei t'o spray deacidification solutions do not involve the handling of wet, weak paper and do not absolutely require a fume hood. Instructions for their use and for the necessary safety precautions are available from the supplier.

Pastel or charcoal drawings should never be encapsulated, as the static electricity of the polyester film might lift some of their particles.

Only outsize materials (particularly subject to mechanical damage when handled) and fragile ones should be encapsulated. ·Polyester film is heavy and a policy of blanket encapsulation can cause a weight problem.

There are, at present, three methods of encapsulation:

    Ultrasonic welding
    Sealing with double-faced tape
    Sewing

Ultrasonic welding is still very expensive.

The original encapsulation process, developed by the Library of Congress, is sealing with double-faced tape. While usually safe and effective, it can cause damage if the material slips so that its edge is caught against the edge of the tape and pieces are pulled away.

Under adverse storage conditions, the adhesive can creep out into the envelope with the same result.

However, both these occurrences are very unlikely and in most cases this method of encapsulation works well. It also has the advantage of being very easy to do.

Put a piece of graph paper on a board such as masonite or binder's board and tape a piece of polyester film on top of it, using the method described on the following pages. This keeps the graph paper clean and intact so that it can be used again and again.

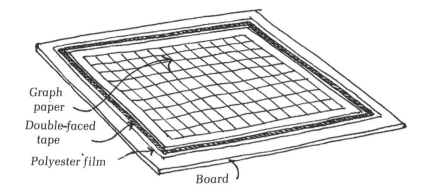

Graph paper

Double-faced tape

Polyester film

Board

If you are going to encapsulate many documents of the same size, mark the position of the tape on the graph paper.

Cut two pieces of polyester film 1" larger than the document on all four sides.

Put one piece of polyester film on the graph paper board and rub it down with a lint-free dust cloth to set up static electricity to hold it in place and remove any dust it may have collected.

Center the document on the polyester film and put a small weight on it.

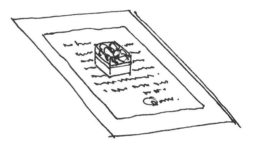

Put the tape down along the lines of the graph paper and about 1/8" away from the document on all four sides.

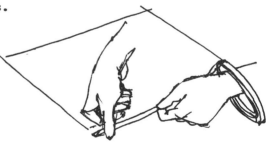

PAPER TREATMENT

Fold the tape back and cut it
off at a right angle with a
scalpel.

Optional gap ↴

A small gap (less than 1/16") may
be left in one corner to allow
air exchange within the envelope,
or it may be completely sealed.

Leave the brown paper on the tape.

Put the other piece of polyester
film down on top of the document,
lining it up with the first piece.

Rub it down with a dust cloth
and put a weight on it.

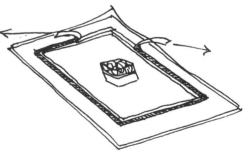

Reach under the top sheet of polyester
film and peel the brown paper off the
tape on two sides of the document.
Smooth the film down.

Repeat with the other two sides.

Rub down along the tape with a
dust cloth.

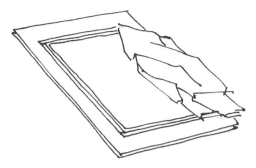

Trim the envelope, leaving a margin
of 1/8" outside the tape on all four
sides. This will prevent the edge
of the tape from picking up dirt.

Sewing has no disadvantages and is the most economical method of encapsulation -- once you have paid for a sewing machine.

A sewing machine may need some adjustment for sewing polyester film.
Give your dealer two pieces of polyester film to try out and ask him or her
to make a suitable adjustment for your machine.

Cut two sheets of polyester film
about 1" larger than the document
on all four sides.

Put the document, centered, between
the two pieces of film.

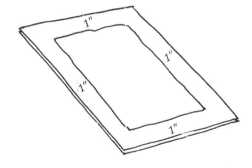

Staple the edges of the film together on two sides.

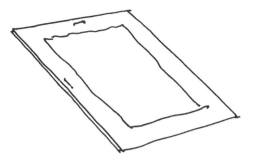

Rub the sandwich with a cloth. This will set up enough static electricity to hold the document in place while you are sewing.

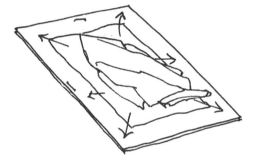

Sew around the document, about 1/8" out from it on all sides, with invisible nylon thread. Start near a corner.

A straight or zigzag sewing stitch can be used. The zigzag is better looking than straight sewing.

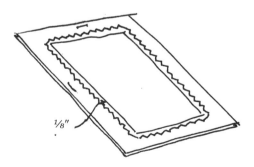

1/8"

BOOKS: THEIR CARE AND REPAIR

Finish off the sewing by overlapping about 1/2". Trim the threads flush.

Trim the edges of the envelope about 1/8" out from the sewing. This will cut off the staples that held the envelope together while it was being sewn.

BOOKPLATING

Bookplates usually curl when pasted and this makes them difficult to handle. They can, however, be flattened before they are pasted.

Wet them with a damp sponge or run water on them and blot them with a paper towel.

In a few minutes the paper will relax, uncurl, and be easy to paste.

It is sometimes necessary to remove bookplates, so paste with a mixture of 25% PVA to 75% methyl cellulose. This makes an adhesive that is easy to remove.

Build up a support of boards (wooden and/or binder's boards) or books, position the bookplate, put a clean waste sheet on it and rub it down.

Put a piece of polyester film or waxed paper over the bookplate to prevent moisture exchange when you close the book.

Let it extend slightly so you won't forget to take it out.

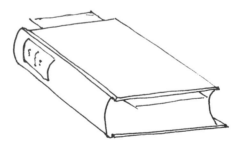

BOOKS: THEIR CARE AND REPAIR

TIP-INS AND POCKETS

These instructions are intended for research materials only -- not for rare books.

"Tipping" is the attachment of one leaf to another by means of a narrow strip of adhesive along one edge. In the context of this chapter, "tip-ins" are materials that need to be added to books already bound -- such as errata slips, indexes, replacements of misprinted pages provided by the publisher, or replacements, usually photocopies, for pages lost, torn, or cut out.

These materials are most frequently in one of four formats each of which requires a different treatment:

> a single leaf
> several single leaves
> a folded sheet
> several folded sheets, one inside another

Pockets are usually adhered to the back board of a book to hold materials that belong with it, but should not be adhered to it, such as large folding maps or groups of loose plates.

It isn't possible to specify the maximum number of leaves (since paper varies so much in thickness) to be tipped in or the maximum thickness of material to be put in a pocket.

Remember that when a book is shelved,

compression here   puts strain here and damages the binding.

You will have to use your own judgment on this point.

If a very large number of leaves are missing from a book, replacement or reproduction is probably the answer.

If very thick material requires a pocket, it can be put in a protective cover with a suitable call number and shelved beside the book itself.

EQUIPMENT

The equipment and materials suggested in these lists are for books under 14" high. Sizes must naturally be increased for larger books.

Cutter or board shears
3 or 4 wooden pressing boards, 9" x 14"
3 or 4 large weights
2 small weights
2 brushes
   2" house painting brush
   1" oil painting brush
Triangle
Straight edge
Bone folder
Scissors
Utility knife or scalpel
Needle, No. 6 crewel
Adhesive container

MATERIALS

The amounts given in parentheses are adequate for about 100 tip-ins or pockets.

Tip-ins:

Waste cardboard (5 or 6 pieces)
Newsprint (1 pad, 18" x 24")
Japanese tissue (2 sheets)
Waxed paper (1 roll)
Linen thread, Barbour's 3 cord, No. 30 (one 50 gram spool)
Beeswax (1 small container)
Adhesive, 50/50 (1 cup)

Pockets:

Paper, preferably acid-free (25 sheets or an 18" x 24" pad of thin
   drawing paper)
Bristol board, .010 (25 sheets or an 18" x 24" pad)
Double-faced tape (3 rolls)

MEASURING

Material to be tipped in usually needs to be trimmed.

Use the tip-in itself in marking for trimming.

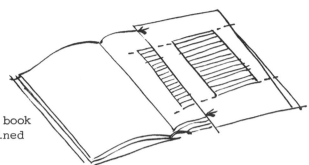

Put the tip-in on the book with the text areas lined up.

Mark the head and tail of the page at the arrows and cut off the excess.

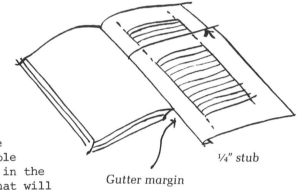

¼" stub

Gutter margin

Do the same with the fore-edge, if possible allowing 1/4" extra in the gutter margin for what will be a stub.

To be sure that the tip-in will not extend beyond the rest of the book, you may want to trim it about 1/16" in from your marks.

After trimming, put the tip-in in position in the book (without adhesive) to check your measurements and to make doubly sure that it will not extend beyond the other pages.

If the gutter margin of material to be tipped in is less than 3/8",
photocopy it with a wider gutter margin.

Trim the tip-in to the size of the
book (or slightly less) at head
tail and fore-edge.

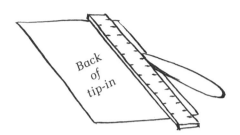

Place a straight edge 1/4" in from
the gutter edge of the tip-in and
score along it with the point of
a bone folder.

Fold the 1/4" around to the
back and rub down the fold
with a bone folder. This
folded edge is called a stub.

Tipping in

Put the tip-in, with the stub out flat,
on a waste pasting strip.
Put another pasting strip on top of it
with its edge lined up with the inner
edge of the stub.

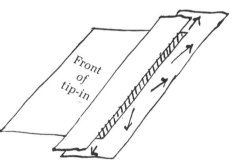

Paste the shaded area in the
direction of the arrows.

Throw away the pasting strips
before proceeding.

BOOKS: THEIR CARE AND REPAIR

Position the tip-in as far into the fold of the book as possible.

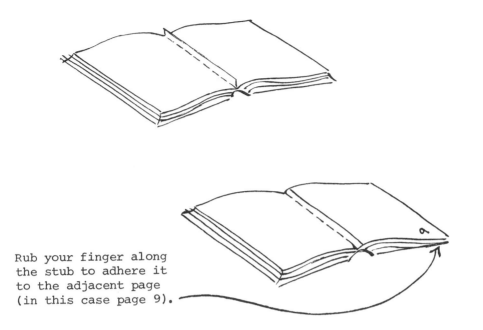

Rub your finger along
the stub to adhere it
to the adjacent page
(in this case page 9).

Put a strip of waxed paper
in the fold to prevent any
excess adhesive from sticking
the stub and the tip-in itself
together.

Put another strip of waxed paper
on the front of the tip-in. Hold
the book open so that the pasted
area is supported and rub gently
along it with a bone folder.

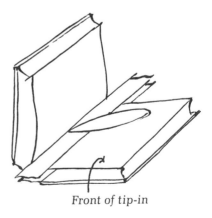

Front of tip-in

Close the book and let it dry for
at least five hours before removing
the waxed paper strips. Overnight
drying is best.

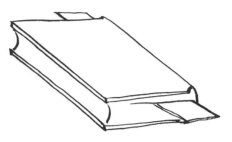

If the tip-in extends beyond the other pages, in spite of all your care,
it should be trimmed flush with them when the tipped edge has dried.

Put a piece of waste board
under the tip-in and cut
off the excess using a
scalpel and straight edge.

ADDED STUB

If the gutter margin of a book is so narrow that a 1/4" edge folded back
to form a stub would obscure text, a transparent stub of Japanese tissue
may be added instead.

To add a stub:

Cut a 1/2" strip of transparent Japanese
tissue to a length slightly greater than
tip-in.

← Grain →

Put the tip-in, front side up, on a
waste strip and put another waste
strip on top of it, leaving 1/4"
of the gutter edge exposed.

Front
of
tip-in

Paste in the direction of the arrows. Throw away the waste sheets.

Put the tip-in on a sheet of waxed paper
and position the strip of Japanese tissue,
lining up its edge with the edge of the
pasted area.

Put another strip of waxed paper
on top of it and rub down with the
flat edge of a bone folder.

*Front
of
tip-in*

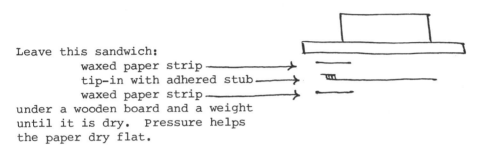

Leave this sandwich:
  waxed paper strip ⟶
  tip-in with adhered stub ⟶
  waxed paper strip ⟶
under a wooden board and a weight
until it is dry. Pressure helps
the paper dry flat.

Trim the Japanese tissue strip flush at head and tail with scissors.

A tip-in with an added stub is tipped into the book in the same way as
is a single leaf.

TIPPING IN SEVERAL SINGLE LEAVES

If the gutter margins of the material to be tipped in are very narrow,
they can be photocopied with wider ones.

Photocopied material can be difficult to trim as the margins may be of
different widths. In that case it is necessary to determine the exact
size of the tip-in and then trim each leaf individually, lining up
margins as best you can.

Trim the last leaf 1/4" wider than the
others if possible, so that it can be
folded back to form a stub.

To join 4 leaves (8 pages):

Place all the leaves except the first
one (pp. 1-2), which needs no adhesive,
on a waste sheet with 1/8" of the gutter
edge of each exposed. Put a waste strip
1/8" in from the edge of the first leaf,
(pp. 3-4).

Paste all the exposed areas at the
same time, pasting in the direction
of the arrows.

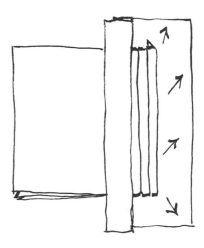

Separate the leaves, which will stick together slightly at the very edge.

Pick up each leaf and line up its edge with the preceding one, adding
the unpasted leaf (pp. 1-2) on top.

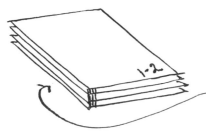

Rub down the adhered edges
with a bone folder.

The adhered leaves may now be treated as a single leaf and tipped into the
book in the same way, with or without an added Japanese tissue stub, depending on the width of the gutter margin.

TIPPING IN MULTIPLE LEAVES

This method is useful if a large number of single leaves need to be
tipped in, and is a better, if more time-consuming, way of attaching
them to each other. It is called "guarding."

To attach 8 leaves (16 pages) together, cut 4 strips of Japanese tissue
1/2" wide and slightly longer than the leaves.

BOOKS: THEIR CARE AND REPAIR

Position the 2 inner leaves
(pp. 7-8 and 9-10) side by side
on a strip of waxed paper. Put
a small weight in the center of
each.

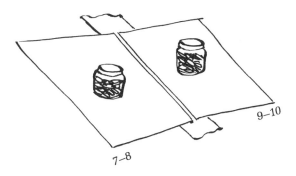

On a waste strip, paste a
Japanese tissue guard, as
usual leaving about 1/2"
at one end unpasted so
that the guard will be
easy to pick up. Put it,
paste side down, along
the center of the 2 leaves.

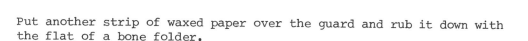

Put another strip of waxed paper over the guard and rub it down with
the flat of a bone folder.

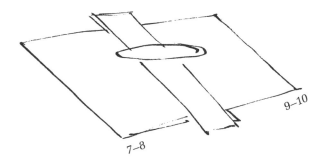

TIP-INS AND POCKETS

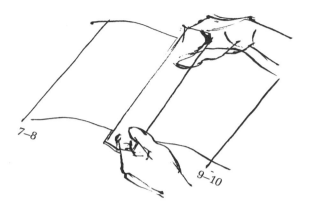

7-8

9-10

Pick up the attached leaves with the waxed paper still in place on each side, and put them aside to dry under a wooden board and a weight.

Repeat the process with the rest of the corresponding pages.

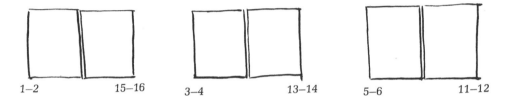

1-2   15-16   3-4   13-14   5-6   11-12

Pile them on top of each other with a strip of waxed paper between each pair and let them dry under the board and the weight for at least 3 hours.

They can then be folded and sewn together.

To attach an uneven number of leaves -- 7, for example -- together, the central leaf, pp. 7-8, should be folded at the gutter edge to form a stub extending about 1/4". If necessary, a stub of Japanese tissue can be added.

Cut 3 strips of Japanese tissue and guard the pages together as follows:

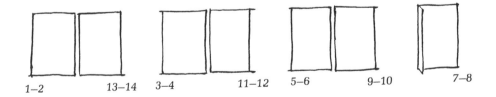

1-2   13-14   3-4   11-12   5-6   9-10   7-8

In sewing through the folds, the stub of pp. 7-8 is treated as if it were a full leaf.

BOOKS: THEIR CARE AND REPAIR

TIPPING IN A SINGLE FOLDED SHEET

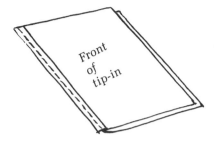

A single folded sheet can have 1/8" pasted along the gutter margin or a stub added and can be tipped in as already described on pp. 94-97.

TIPPING IN SEVERAL FOLDED SHEETS

These sheets, often stapled together when they are received, can be sewn together through their folds rather than adhered.

Remove the staples.

Cut a strip of Japanese tissue about 3/4" wide and the height of the tip-in. Fold it in half around the outside of the folded sheets.

A thread about 2-1/2 times the height of the tip-in is needed.

Start sewing inside the fold, leaving a tail of thread long enough to tie in a knot.

Sew in the direction of the arrows, ending in the middle, where you started.

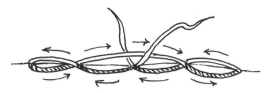

▧ Outside fold

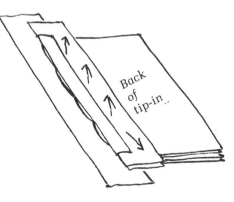

Tie a square knot (left over right, right over left) around the long center stitch.

Trim the ends of the thread, leaving about 1/4".

Put the tip-in on a waste strip with a piece of waxed paper and a waste strip underneath the sewn guard.

Paste in the direction of the arrows, avoiding the threads (which tend to collect excess adhesive) as much as possible.

Back of tip-in

Remove the waste strip but leave the waxed paper in place.

Tip in as already described.

BOOKS: THEIR CARE AND REPAIR

Torn edges can be trimmed somewhat by putting a thin piece of board --
such as shirt cardboard -- underneath them and cutting away the parts
that protrude farthest.

Do not try to cut out the remaining stubs as they are holding their
conjugate leaves in the binding.

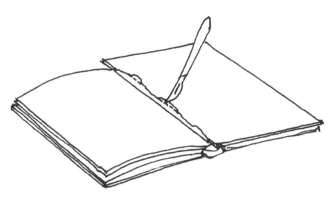

It is almost always necessary to add a
transparent stub to the tip-in, as it
can only butt up to the torn or cut
edge and so must be adhered over the
text.

If margins are so narrow that text will
extend beyond the book at the fore-edge,
the material to be tipped in can be
photocopied, reduced by 1/3.

TIP-INS AND POCKETS

POCKETS

A pocket, to be placed inside the back cover, can be made for material that belongs with a book but should not be attached to it -- a folding map, for example.

Materials more than 1/4" thick should never be added to a bound book as this will strain the binding.

If the material to go in the pocket is fragile, it can be wrapped in a piece of paper, preferably acid-free paper such as "Permalife."

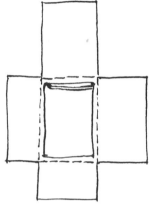

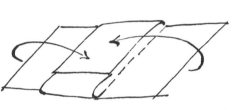

Cut a rectangle of Bristol board, grain long, so that its width is equal to the width of the book's cover board plus 2" and its height is 1-2/3 the height of the book's cover board.

These measurements need not be precise, so measure by eye.

Score the Bristol with a bone folder at a right angle to the edge.

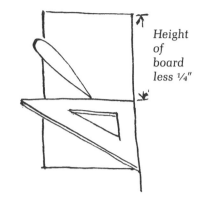

Height of board less ¼"

Fold the Bristol.

Cut away the shaded areas with a scalpel and straight edge.

2"

Score and fold the small flap.

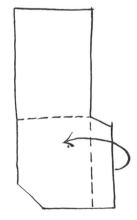

Cut 2 strips of double-faced tape down on the small flap.

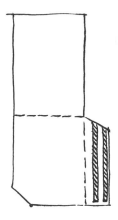

Put the material on the Bristol and fold the lower flap up and the small flap around to the back.

Leave the material in place.

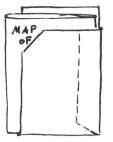

Turn the pocket over and remove the brown paper from the tape.

Press the small flap down.

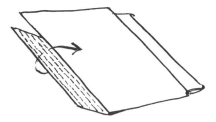

Put 3 strips of double-faced tape, short of the edges, on the back of the pocket.

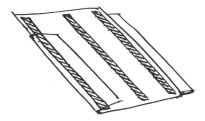

BOOKS: THEIR CARE AND REPAIR

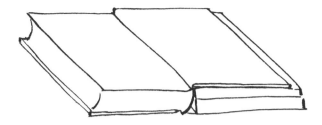

Support the board.
(Other books may be used.)

Remove the brown paper and
position the pocket about
1/8" in from the fore-edge
and tail.

Press down firmly.

* *

If the material is thick,
make two folds far enough
apart to accommodate the
thickness, instead of the
single folds just described.

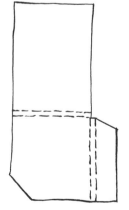

TIP-INS AND POCKETS

PAMPHLET BINDING

In this context pamphlets are regarded as printed matter, under 1/2" thick, bound into a limp cover. Because their covers are limp, pamphlets need some form of hard-cover protection, but because there are so many of them, covers must be simple and easy to attach.

Pamphlet material varies in its makeup, as follows:

Single-signature

Folded pieces of paper are placed one inside another and stapled or sewn through the fold to a limp cover.

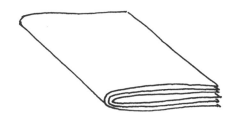

Identification: Staples or sewing threads are visible along the outer fold and in the center of the signature.

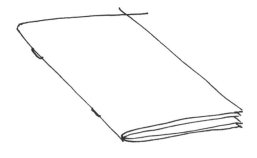

Multiple-signature

Several groups of folded pieces of paper placed one inside another are sewn together through the folds.

A limp cover is then glued around them.

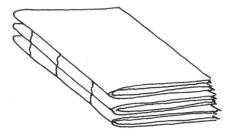

BOOKS: THEIR CARE AND REPAIR

Identification: The folds are visible at the head and tail of the binding edge; the threads can be seen in the center of each signature.

Adhesive-bound

Several single sheets of paper are glued together at the spine.

A limp cover is then glued around them.

Identification: The single sheets and a layer of adhesive are visible at the head and tail of the binding edge. There is no sewing thread.

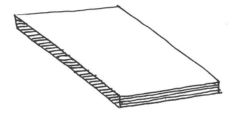

As already explained, books, including pamphlets, are usually printed on large sheets of paper which are then folded. In most adhesive bindings, the folds are cut off before the leaves are glued together.

In some adhesive bindings cuts are made along the folds allowing adhesive to penetrate and hold the folded sheets together. These books look as if they were sewn through the fold, but the absence of sewing threads inside the pamphlet will make identification as an adhesive binding sure.

PAMPHLET BINDING

Side-stapled

Some material consists entirely of single sheets, including two side-stapled cover sheets.

Identification is never difficult.

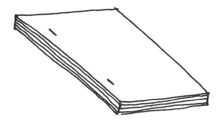

In other cases the bookblock itself is stapled and a cover is then glued around it.

Identification: The staples can be felt on the sides of the pamphlet.

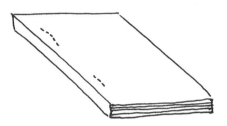

Each makeup requires a different type of treatment -- all of these will be described.

EQUIPMENT

Cutter or board shears
Electric drill and drill guide (optional)
Drill bits
Pressing boards
Weights, large
2 brushes:
   2" house painting brush
   1" oil painting brush
Needles:
   4" mattress needle
   No. 3 darning needle
   No. 6 crewel needle

PAMPHLET BINDING

Utility knife or scalpel
Straight edge
Potter's cut-off needle
Stapler
Kitchen knife, dull
Bone folder
Scissors
Adhesive containers
Paper clips

MATERIALS

The amounts given in parentheses are adequate for about 100 pamphlet covers.

Board
    Acid-free board is available in various thicknesses -- .020 and .040 (lig-free) and .050 (barrier board) -- and in various sizes (25-75 depending on the size of the pamphlets and the board).

    If you plan to buy board in sheets and cut it yourself, remember that the narrower dimension of the board should be slightly less than the blade of your cutter knife.

    Board is also available cut to sizes such as:

                        6" x 9"
                        8" x 11"
                        9" x 12"
                       12" x 18"
                       14" x 24"

    Various types of pamphlet folders are also available in these or similar sizes.

Bristol board, .010, acid-free (30 sheets)
Bookcloth, buckram (5 yds.)
Linen thread, Barbour's 3 cord, Nos. 18 and 30 (one 50 gram spool of each)
Linen cord, Fawcett's Penn-Made, 6 cord and 10 cord (1 lb. of each)
Staples (1 box)
Newsprint (1 pad)
Waxed paper (1 roll)
Adhesive, 50/50 (1 pt.)

PAMPHLET BINDING

As already mentioned, the easiest ways to measure are with the objects themselves or with a strip of paper.

To measure for a pamphlet cover, line up the pamphlet with the edges of the board.

Mark any needed additions or subtractions in width or height by eye or, if you must, with a ruler.

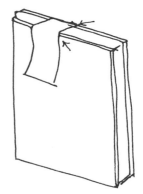

Measure thickness with a strip of paper.

You will need to use the measuring unit board thickness (BT), which varies with the board you are using, in measuring for pamphlet covers.

Precise measurements are given in the following instructions as guidelines only.

If you are using boards cut to standard sizes, use the size that is slightly larger than your pamphlet, even if it doesn't fit precisely. Of course, if you want to take the time you can cut the boards to size.

BOOKS: THEIR CARE AND REPAIR

The staples of most single-signature pamphlets are made of galvanized iron, which will eventually rust.

To remove staples:

Bend up the legs with a dull kitchen knife.

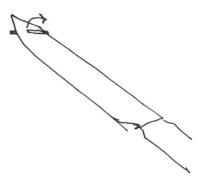

Pry out the staple with a see-saw motion.

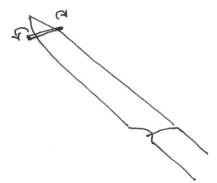

Cut a piece of bookcloth 2" wide by the height of the pamphlet and fold it in half around the pamphlet, with the right side of the cloth in.

The dull side of the cloth is the right side.

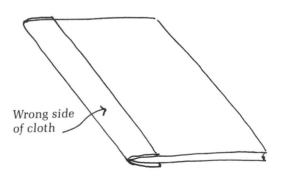

Wrong side of cloth

Sew the pamphlet to the
hinge in the way described
for sewing the several folded
sheets of a tip-in to a Japanese tissue hinge. See pp.
101-102.

The outside of the pamphlet
will look like this.

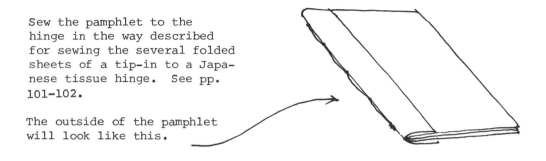

Very Thick Single-Signature Pamphlet

If the pamphlet is very thick you will
find it easier to punch the sewing
holes with an awl or a potter's
cut-off needle before starting
to sew.

Increase the number of sewing holes
to seven and use the same sewing
pattern.

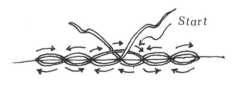

Start

To make a cover, cut 2 boards
the width of the pamphlet by
the height plus 1/4".

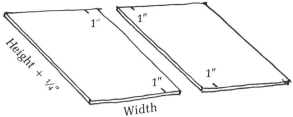

Mark off 1" at the head and
tail of each board with a pencil.

The width of the strip of cloth for the spine depends on the thickness
of the pamphlet.

The distance between the boards should be: the thickness of the pamphlet
plus 2 BT's plus 1/4".

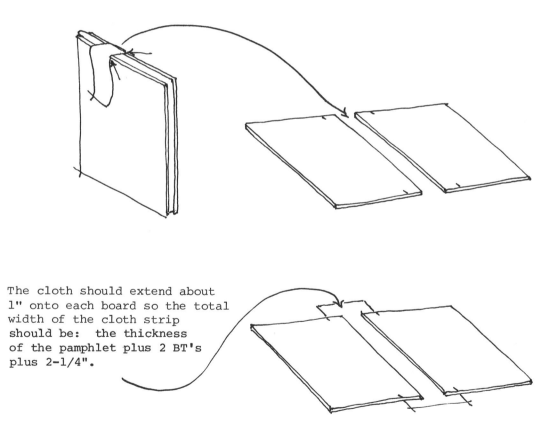

The cloth should extend about
1" onto each board so the total
width of the cloth strip
should be: the thickness
of the pamphlet plus 2 BT's
plus 2-1/4".

PAMPHLET BINDING

Cut a strip of cloth the width
just described by the height
of the boards plus 1".

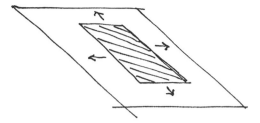

Glue the cloth on a waste sheet
in the direction of the arrows.

Throw away the waste sheet, and
then position the boards on the
glued cloth, lining up the pencil
marks with the edge of the cloth.

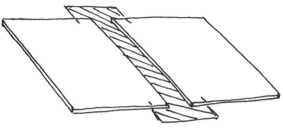

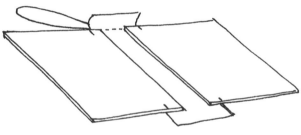

Turn the cloth tightly around
the boards, rubbing along the
edge of the boards with a bone
folder.

Work the cloth down between
the boards, also with a bone
folder.

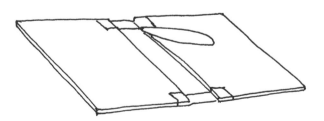

BOOKS: THEIR CARE AND REPAIR

Fold the sewn cloth
hinge out flat.

Put one waste sheet between it and
the pamphlet and another under the
extending portion.

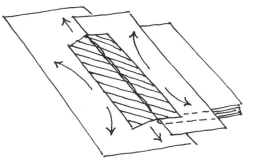

Paste in the direction of the arrows,
pasting lightly over the sewing
threads and very lightly and carefully at each end.

Center the fold of the pamphlet
on the fold of the cover and
rub down the cloth on each
side with a bone folder.

Work the cloth down between
the boards.

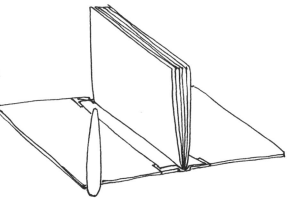

Put a strip of waxed paper on either
side of the pamphlet, inside the
boards and the cloth hinges you
have just glued, to act as a moisture
barrier.

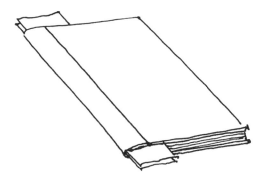

Let the pamphlet dry overnight
under a board and a weight.

MULTIPLE-SIGNATURE PAMPHLET

Cut a piece of bookcloth so that its
height is the same as the pamphlet's
and its width 2" greater.

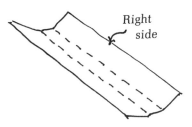

Right
side

Fold it to the thickness of the spine
with the right side in and rub down
the folds with a bone folder.

Find the center of the first
signature, or if the first
signature has very few pages
in it (which is often the
case), that of the second.

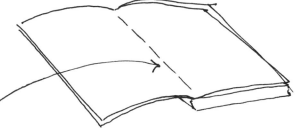

The sewing threads in the
center of each signature
look like this.

BOOKS: THEIR CARE AND REPAIR

Position the cloth on the spine
of the pamphlet and attach it
to the center of the first and
last signatures with paper clips.

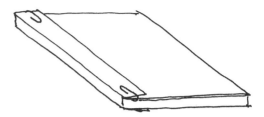

Sewing is made easier by punching
holes with a small awl or a potter's
cut-off needle.

Punch through the original
sewing holes at the head and
tail of the pamphlet.

The holes should go through the
signature you are about to sew
into only and should not angle
down through the other signatures
of the pamphlet.

Sew with a waxed thread
three times as long as
the pamphlet.

Use No. 30 thread for small,
light pamphlets, No. 18 for
large, heavy ones.

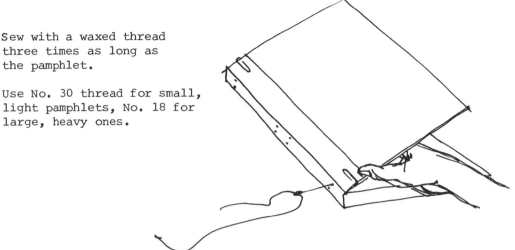

Sew in and out of the fold following this diagram, crossing over to
the last signature and sewing back along it in the same way.

Cross over to where you started and tie a square knot.

Cut the threads, leaving about 1/4".

Square knot

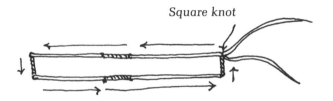

The sewn hinge will look like
this.

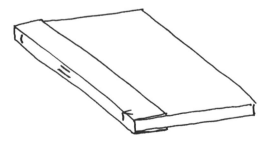

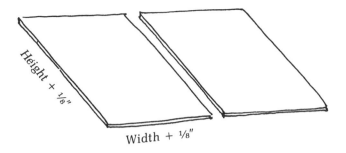

The materials needed for the cover are 2 boards cut to the width of the pamphlet plus 1/8" and to the height plus 1/8".

Also needed is a piece of bookcloth, cut to the thickness of the pamphlet plus 2" and to the height of the boards plus 1".

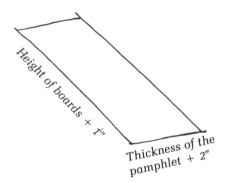

The cover is made in the same way as that for a single-signature pamphlet. See pp. 115-117.

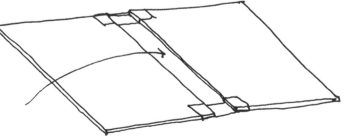

Place the boards so that the distance between them is the thickness of the pamphlet plus 2 BT's plus 1/8".

Position the pamphlet in the case, flush at the tail, and with the edge of the spine extending about 1/16" beyond the back board.

Put a waxed paper strip and a waste strip under the front hinge. Glue the hinge with PVA slightly diluted with water but not mixed with methyl cellulose. Remove the waste strip, leaving the waxed paper in place, and fold the front board tightly around the pamphlet.

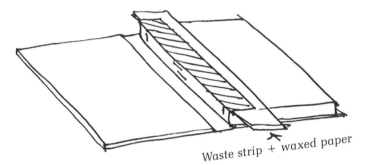

Waste strip + waxed paper

Repeat with the back hinge.

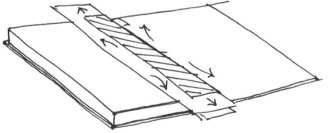

In binding flush at the tail, a heavy bookblock and its cover will support each other. Although the tail of the pamphlet may get dirty, a little dirt is better than a binding attachment that is pulling apart.

BOOKS: THEIR CARE AND REPAIR

Press down on the hinge area with the palms of your hands.

Let the pamphlet dry overnight under a board and a weight.

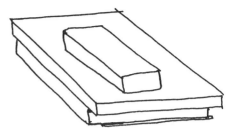

ADHESIVE-BOUND OR SIDE-STAPLED PAMPHLET

Most contemporary pamphlets are bound this way.

The materials needed for the cover are 2 boards: the width of the pamphlet less 3/16" by the height plus 1/4".

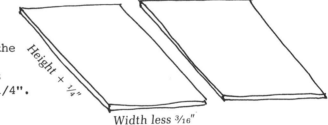

Height + ¼"

Width less ³⁄₁₆″

A piece of bookcloth: the thickness of the pamphlet plus 2" by the height of the boards plus 1".

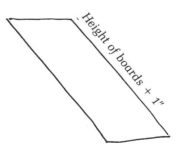

Height of boards + 1"

Thickness of the pamphlet + 2"

The distance between the boards
is the thickness of the pamphlet
plus 2 BT's plus 5/8".

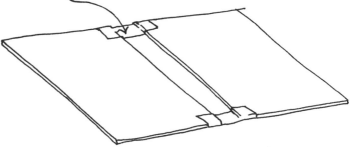

The cover is made in the same way as that of a single-signature pamphlet, with one exception.

Only a little more than 1" on each
long edge of the cloth is glued or
the adhesive in the cloth area is
allowed to dry before the next step
is taken.

This prevents adhesive from getting
on the pamphlet itself.

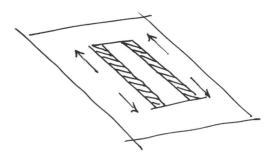

Put the pamphlet into the cover
with its spine tight against
the cloth at the spine of the
cover.

Put one or two pieces of waste board
underneath it to protect the bench
when you drill, and a weight on top
of it.

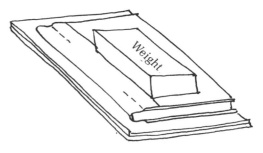

BOOKS: THEIR CARE AND REPAIR

Drill three holes, one approximately
in the middle of the pamphlet
and one about 1" in from
each end.

They should be about 3/16"
in from the spine.

Be careful to avoid the staples if you
have not removed them.

Use a piece of cord three
times as long as the
pamphlet for sewing.

Wax the cord thoroughly.

Sew according to this diagram:

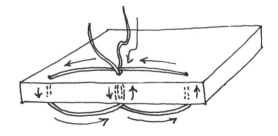

Tie a square knot around the
long stitch and trim the ends,
leaving about 1/2".

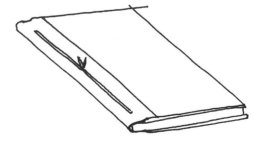

It is difficult to sew material exceeding 13" in length with a single cord.

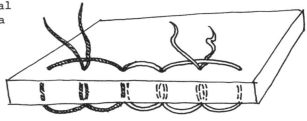

If very large materials are to be put into a cover, use one piece of cord for one half and another for the other half, with one hole used for both.

Increase the number of sewing holes to 8 or 10 depending on the height of the material.

UNBINDABLE MATERIAL

Some materials are too fragile to tolerate any kind of attachment. Others, such as maps too large to fit in a pocket inside the board of the book or loose plates, are also unbindable but need a protective cover.

A pocket within an outer cover can be made for such materials.

The pocket consists of a piece of 2-ply Bristol board folded in half.

The grain of the Bristol is not important, although it will fold more easily if the grain is parallel to the fold.

The pocket is less likely to bulge if the grain is at a right angle to the fold.

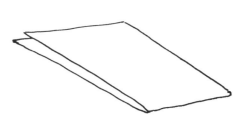

BOOKS: THEIR CARE AND REPAIR

The dimensions of the pocket
depend on the thickness of the
material it is designed to hold.

If the material is thin, cut the
folded Bristol board so that it
is 1" larger in height and width.

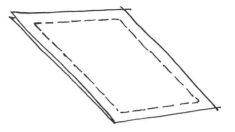

If the material is thin, cut the
folded Bristol board so that
it is at least 2-1/2" larger
in height and width.

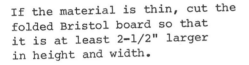

The materials needed for the outer cover are 2 boards: the width of the
folded Bristol plus 1/4" by its height plus 1/4".

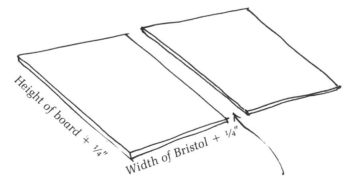

The distance between the boards is the thickness of the material,
including the Bristol pocket and the boards themselves.

Take two pieces of bookcloth: cut one - the outer cloth - so it measures the distance between the boards plus 2" by their height plus 1". Cut the spine lining so it measures the distance between the boards plus 1" by the height of the boards less 1/4".

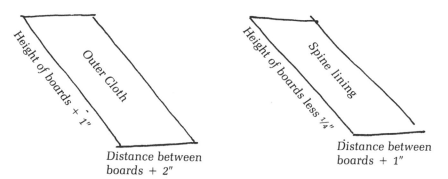

Make a case like that for a multiple-signature pamphlet (p. 118) with the addition of a spine lining. Work the spine lining down along the edges of the boards in the spine area.

Staple the folded Bristol to the cover, flush at the fore-edge and centered at head and tail.

Cut a piece of bookcloth the height of the folded Bristol by 2" and glue and adhere it around the cover and the Bristol so that the staples will not abrade an adjacent book on the shelf.

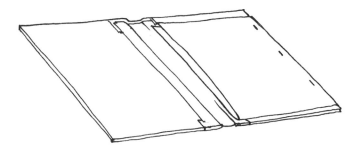

HINGE AND JOINT REPAIR

These instructions are not intended for rare books or historically or artistically valuable bindings, but for commercially produced, cloth case bindings such as those in common use today.

As explained earlier, a case binding is one in which the leaves of the book are linked by sewing or adhesion and then attached to a protective cover made separately.

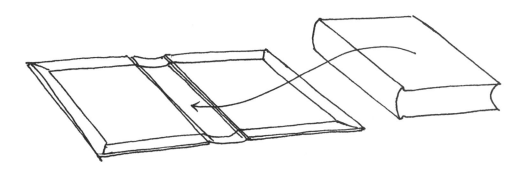

The repairs described in this chapter are all concerned with breakdowns in the area where the bookblock is attached to the case.

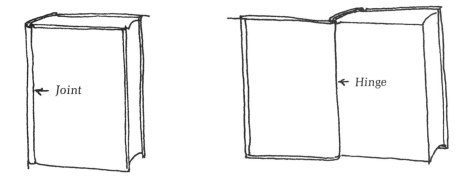

This area is called a joint on the outside and a hinge on the inside. It is the weakest part of any binding and so most often in need of repair.

The attachment between bookblock and case is made up of two layers of material:

1. A folded piece of paper called an endsheet, sometimes reinforced with cloth at the fold.

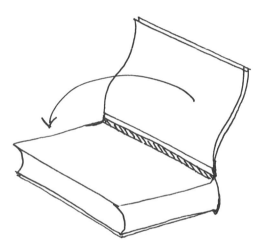

It is glued to the book for about 1/4" along the shoulder.

2. A piece of coursely woven cloth called "super" or "mull," is glued to the spine of the bookblock and extends (or should) about 1" on either side of it.

The extending parts of the spine lining and 1/2 of each folded endsheet are adhered to the inside of the case.

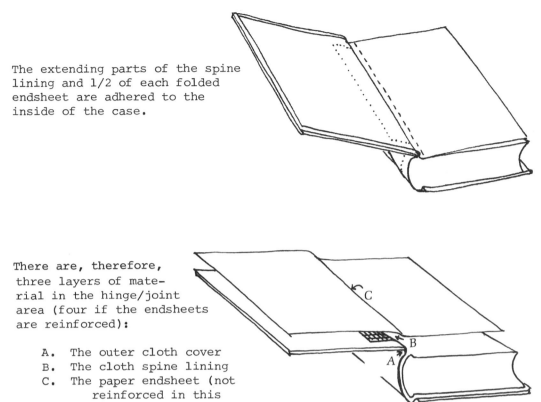

There are, therefore, three layers of material in the hinge/joint area (four if the endsheets are reinforced):

    A.   The outer cloth cover
    B.   The cloth spine lining
    C.   The paper endsheet (not reinforced in this diagram).

Although this seems like a strong attachment, continual use of the book, poor quality materials and binding practices, or the weight of the book-block or the boards of the case can, and frequently do, cause any or all of these materials to break or pull apart.

This chapter describes hinge and joint repairs but not complete rebinding, which is best left to a professional binder.

EQUIPMENT

Cutter or board shears
2 presses (useful but not absolutely necessary)

3 or 4 wooden pressing boards slightly larger than the books you are working on
3 or 4 large weights
2 brushes
    1-1/2" or 2" house painting brush
    1" oil painting brush
Triangle
Straight edge
Utility knife or scalpel
Scissors
Bone folder
Adhesive containers
2 knitting needles
Plastic bottle with a pointed top

Ideally, two types of press are used for these repairs:

A nipping or letter press to exert pressure on the sides of a book. See p. 38.

A board and bricks or several books may be substituted for this type of press.

A lying press which holds the spine of the book up and allows you to exert pressure on it. See p. 39.

A board pressed firmly down with your hand may be substituted, although it is not as easy to work on a spine lying sideways as it is on one that is facing up.

BOOKS: THEIR CARE AND REPAIR

The amounts given in parentheses are sufficient for about 100 repairs.

Adhesives
    PVA, polyvinyl acetate emulsion (2 qts.)
    50/50 (1 qt.)
    Wheat or cornstarch paste (1/2 to 1 lb.)
Bookcloth, buckram, and a lighter cloth, such as Joanna Western Oxford
    for small books and hinges (4 yds. of each)
Muslin or super (3 yds.)
Paper, acid-free or of moderately good quality, such as that available
    in art supply stores (5 sheets of Permalife text or 1 pad of a paper
    such as Strathmore 400)
    Japanese tissue, Kizukishi or Usumino (2 or 3 sheets)
    Newsprint (1 pad 18" by 24") or old newspapers
    Waxed paper (1 roll)
Waste cardboard (5 or 6 sheets)
Cotton swabs or Q-tips (1 box)
Fine sandpaper (6 sheets)
Ace bandage

Measuring

Measure with a strip of paper as described on p. 27.

REINFORCEMENT OF FLYLEAVES

REINFORCEMENT

A cloth hinge adhered to a brittle
piece of paper may cause the paper
to break along the edge of the
cloth.

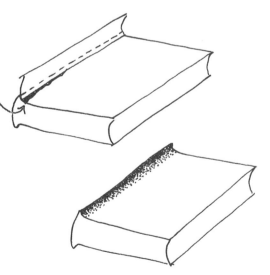

The reinforcement provided by a torn
Japanese tissue strip is gradual,
starting with individual fibers and
ending with the thin, flexible
tissue itself.

If a tissue strip extending farther
than the cloth is adhered before the
cloth itself, a break is less likely.

Paste with wheat or cornstarch paste.

HINGE AND JOINT REPAIR

Hinges usually break because the cloth spine lining is pulling away from the case. Repairing the paper alone does not solve the problem.

Cut through the spine lining in the front and back of the book with a scalpel, being careful not to cut through the outer case.

In many cases only the front hinge breaks. This means that the back hinge is weak and will probably break soon. An added reason for mending both hinges is that it is easier to mend both than it is to mend one.

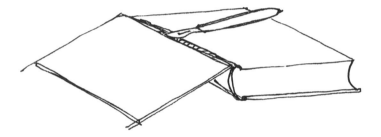

Trim away any excess paper or spine lining that extends beyond the boards at the spine.

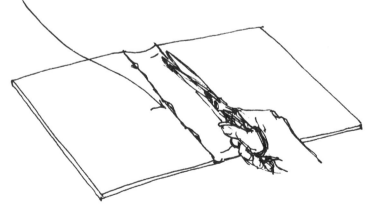

A piece of paper covering the whole spine is usually glued on top of the cloth spine lining. If this is stuck tightly to the spine, leave it in place.

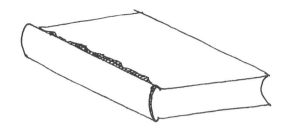

Although the cloth spine lining is usually tightly stuck to the bookblock, the paper spine lining often is not, and any loose parts should be removed.

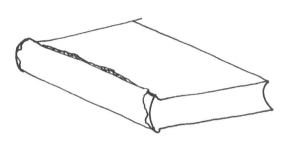

Pull off loose parts with your fingers and sand the spine down with fine sandpaper, being careful not to sand through the cloth spine lining underneath.

The reason for sanding is that the poor quality paper usually used for spine linings can delaminate, pull away from the spine, or turn to mush when wet with adhesive (as it is about to be).

Headbands embroidered on cloth tape, if any, are easily pulled off and can be glued back on when you are relining the spine.

Trim the spine lining along the shoulders of the bookblock.

Be very careful not to cut any paper of the bookblock itself.

If the paper of the first and last flyleaves is brittle, reinforce it with Japanese tissue before adding cloth hinges. See p. 137.

Cut 2 strips of thin bookcloth 1" wide (1-1/4" wide for **very** large books) and the length of the bookblock.

Fold 1/4" over with the right side of the cloth inside the fold.

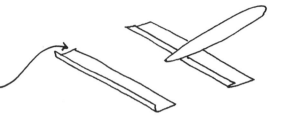

Put a waste strip 1/4" away from the edge of the shoulder and glue the exposed area. Glue in the direction of the arrows.

Throw away the waste strip.

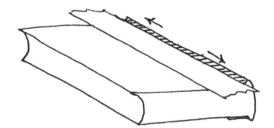

Position the cloth strip, lining up the edge of the fold with the edge of the shoulder. <u>They must be lined up exactly or this repair will not work</u>.

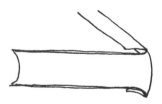

Repeat on the other side of the book.

Wrong side of cloth

BOOKS: THEIR CARE AND REPAIR

Rub the cloth into the
hinge area with a
bone folder.

If you think there is excess
glue extending out from the edge
of the hinge, slip a strip of waxed
paper between the hinge and the bookblock
before rubbing down.

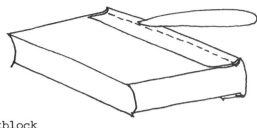

Cut a piece of muslin 1" shorter than the length of the
spine and 2" wider than the spine.

Glue the spine with
50/50 and center the
muslin on it. Rub the
muslin down well with a
bone folder.

This is best done in a **press**,
as a good deal of pressure can
be exerted when rubbing down.
However, it can also be done
with the book on its side.
See p. 132.

Put a waste strip under the
hinge on top of a strip of
waxed paper and glue the
hinge.

Remove the waste sheet but leave
the waxed paper in place.

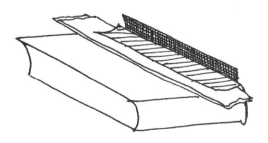

Bring the extending portion of the spine
lining around and down onto the glued
hinge. Rub down.

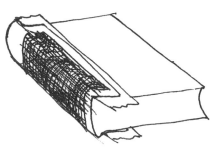

Turn the book over and put it down
on a strip of waxed paper so that
it won't stick to the bench. Glue
the back hinge.

Let the hinges dry for five or ten minutes
with the book extending over the edge
of the bench.

The bookblock and the case can now be put back together.

Position the book on the back board,
lining it up with the pastedown. Be
sure that you are putting it into
the case right side up.

Put a waste strip under the hinge
on top of the waxed paper.

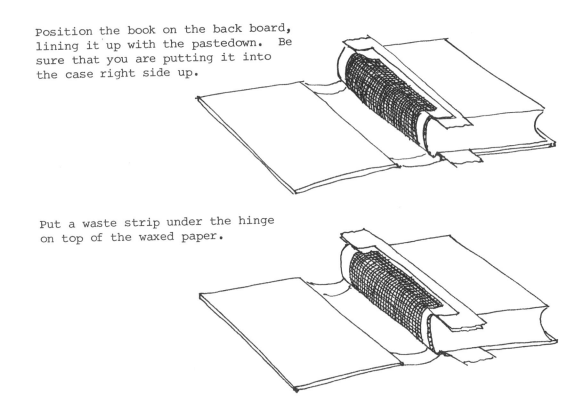

BOOKS: THEIR CARE AND REPAIR

Glue the shaded area (the hinge and the extending part of the spine lining adhered to it) with PVA. Do not glue the spine itself.

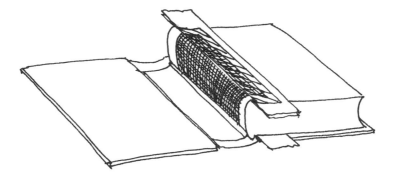

Throw the waste strip away, leaving the waxed paper strip in place.

Bring the board around, pulling the spine of the case tightly around the bookblock. Press down on the board along the hinge.

The front board is now adhered.

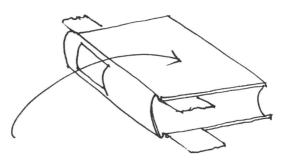

Turn the book over carefully and repeat the process with the back board.

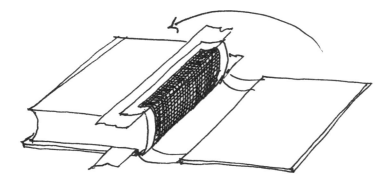

HINGE AND JOINT REPAIR

Work the cloth of the case into
the groove of the joint with a
bone folder.

Put the book in a press between
wooden boards, their edges lined
up with the spine edges of the
boards of the case.

Loosen the press slightly after
about ten minutes. Let the book
dry in the press overnight or
let it dry between boards under
weights -- bricks or heavy books.

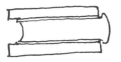

Case and bookblock pulled apart

The case and bookblock frequently pull
apart or break, but the flyleaf and
perhaps a few other leaves remain
attached to the case.

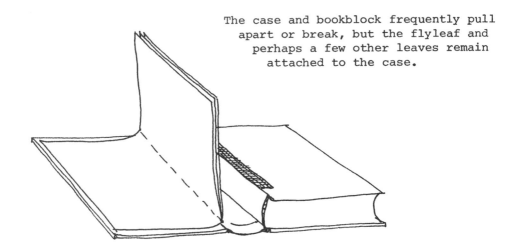

BOOKS: THEIR CARE AND REPAIR

Hold the attached
leaves down firmly
and slit along the
fold as if you were
opening an envelope.

These leaves need to be
reattached to the bookblock.

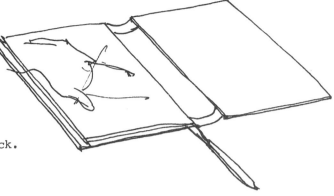

Glue about 1/4" along the hinge
and position the adjacent leaf.
Glue on top of this and add the
next -- and so on.

Be sure the leaves line up at
head, tail, and fore-edge before
rubbing down.

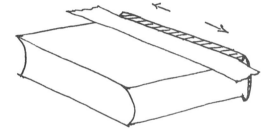

Otherwise the procedure is the same as that described on pp. 134-140.

HEAVY BOOKBLOCKS

Very heavy bookblocks usually
fall forward, away from the
case, so that the tail rests
on the shelf.

Obviously, this weakens or
breaks the hinges and/or
joints.

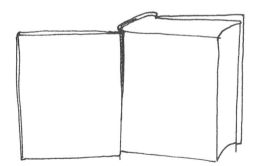

Books can be put back in their case flush at the tail instead of lined up with the pastedown. Remove the headband at the tail if there is one, otherwise follow the instructions on pp. 134-140.

This looks somewhat
peculiar because the
boards extend twice as
much as usual at the head.

However, case and book-
block support each other
so hinges and joints
are much less likely
to break again.

FLAPPING SPINE

It sometimes happens that the
cloth of the outer case breaks,
leaving its spine flapping or
off but with the boards still
firmly attached to the bookblock
by the inner hinge.

If the spine is still attached,
cut it away from the case
with scissors.

BOOKS: THEIR CARE AND REPAIR

Trim away any excess cloth
along the edges of the boards,
being careful not to cut into
the inner hinge material.

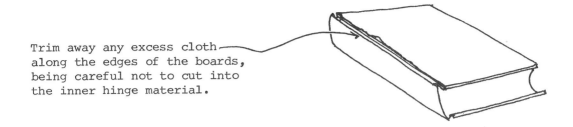

Wrap a strip of newsprint tightly
around the spine of the book and
mark the edge of each board on it.
It is not necessary to work the
strip down into the groove.

Add 1" on either side.

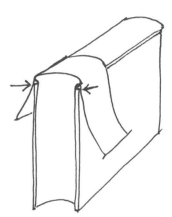

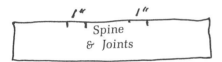

Cut a piece of cloth so that one
dimension measures the width of
the spine and joints plus 2" and
the other dimension measures the
height of the boards plus 1-1/4".

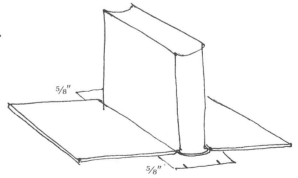

Put the cloth on the book,
centered at head and tail,
and crease it over the edges
of the boards.

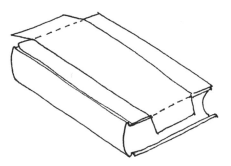

Use the measuring strip to mark the
spine and hinge width, centered, on
each end of the piece of cloth.

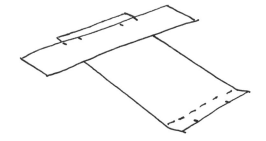

Cut V-shaped slits at these marks,
cutting in just short of the crease.

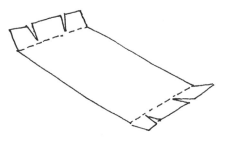

HINGE AND JOINT REPAIR

An inlay of good quality, fairly stiff paper is needed to stiffen the cloth of the spine area.

Cut a strip of paper
the length of the boards
and the width of the spine,
or a hair narrower. The
grain should be long.

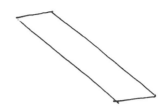

Use a measuring strip to obtain
these measurements.

Glue the inlay.

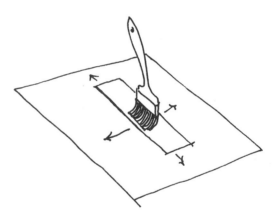

Center it on the cloth.

Put a piece of waxed paper
over it and rub down with
the flat of a bone folder.

Rubbing directly on damp
paper can damage its surface,
and waxed paper is suggested as
it will not stick to any excess
adhesive that may remain on
the edges of the paper strip.

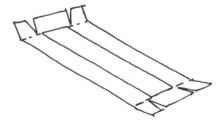

HINGE AND JOINT REPAIR

Put the cloth on a waste sheet and
glue the ends of the spine area.

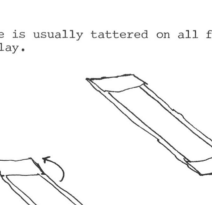

Turn them in around the ends of the
inlay and rub them down .

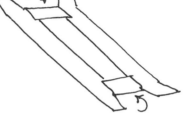

The spine of the original case is usually tattered on all four edges,
with turn-ins stuck to the inlay.

Unfold the turn-ins.

BOOKS: THEIR CARE AND REPAIR

There are various ways of getting the original inlay off the cloth.

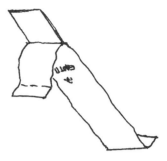

It can often be peeled off. Try bending the cloth away from the inlay and then pulling the two apart.

If this doesn't work, try dampening the inlay and scraping with a scalpel.

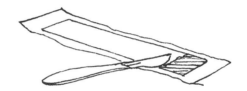

This is a sticky, messy job and the cloth will probably curl up as a result. However, it will flatten when it is glued.

If this doesn't work either, leave the inlay in place.

When the inlay is off, or as much as you can get it, trim the spine so that it is slightly smaller than the new inlay you adhered to your piece of cloth.

Use a scalpel and a straight edge and cut on a piece of waste board.

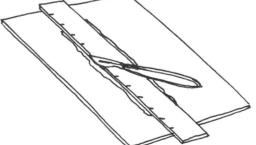

Glue the spine on a waste sheet
and center it on the right side
of the lined cloth.

Rub it down with the flat of a
bone folder.

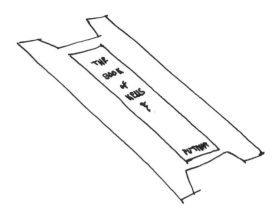

Fold the cloth around the spine
of the bookblock. Be sure the
old spine is centered.

Mark the edge of the cloth.

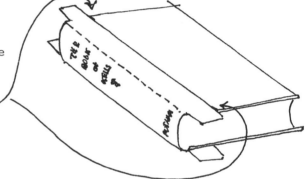

Put a waste strip on the book,
lined up with the marks and
glue the shaded area.

Run your finger along the shoulder
of the bookblock to remove any
excess adhesive.

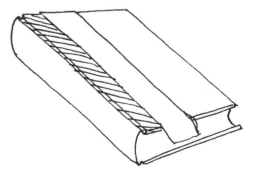

BOOKS: THEIR CARE AND REPAIR

Be sure the text is right side up
in relation to the spine on the
cloth.

Position the cloth, centered at
head and tail and with the edge
lined up with the marks.
Rub down with a bone folder.

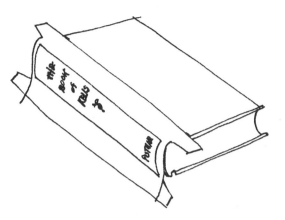

Turn the book over and wrap the
cloth tightly around onto the back
board.

Mark the edges of the cloth at head
and tail.

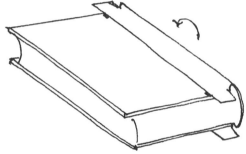

Line up a waste strip with the
marks and glue the shaded area.

Remove the waste strip and
bring the cloth around onto
the glued area. Rub down.

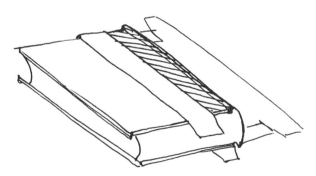

HINGE AND JOINT REPAIR

If the cloth does not fit tightly
around the spine of the bookblock,
work it into the grooves at the
joints with the tip of a bone
folder.

This may not be necessary and the
bookblock will be held firmly in
the case even if this is not done.

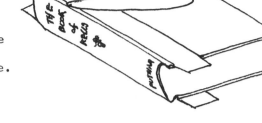

Support the book board with wooden ones or other books.

Glue the extending tabs and fold them around onto the inside of the
boards. Rub down.

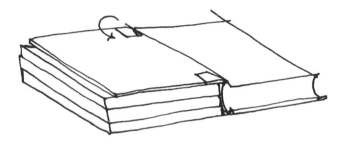

Put a strip of waxed paper along
the hinges on either side of the
book to prevent moisture exchange
from the tabs to the bookblock.

Put the book between wooden boards,
the spine edges of the book boards
lined up with the edges of the
wooden ones.

Let the book dry overnight in a
press or under weights.

BOOKS: THEIR CARE AND REPAIR

If the joints are weak, cut the case apart, cutting along the spine edge of the boards.

Trim ragged edges with scissors. This is much easier than when only the hinge is broken and the case is intact.

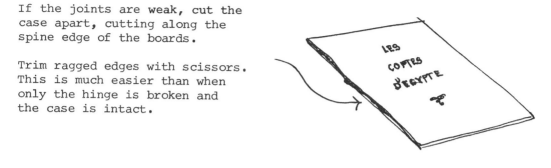

Add hinges and spine linings to the bookblock as described on pp. 136-138.

Cut a piece of cloth the height of the boards plus 1-1/4" (5/8" at head and tail) by the width of the spine and joints plus 2" (see p. 143). Then, cut an inlay the height of the boards by the width of the spine less a hair (see p. 145).

Mark 1" in from the spine edge of the lower board at head and tail.

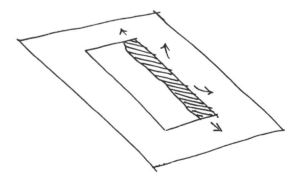

Glue about 1" of the cloth on a waste sheet.

HINGE AND JOINT REPAIR

Position it on the board, centered head and tail, and lined up with the 1" marks.

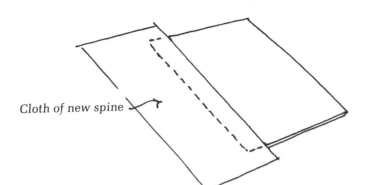

Cloth of new spine

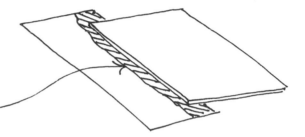

Wipe away any excess adhesive along the long edge of the board.

Put the book on the board, lined up with the pastedown, and put the upper board on the book.

Be sure the boards are lined up at the tail. Check this with a triangle.

BOOKS: THEIR CARE AND REPAIR

Put the paper inlay
in beside the book. This
is only to allow for its
thickness when you wrap the
cloth around it.

Glue the extending edge of
the cloth on a waste sheet and
fold it snugly around onto the
front board, holding the board
firmly in place.

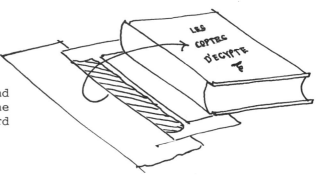

Open out the case and remove the bookblock and the inlay.
Glue the cloth between the boards and at head and tail.

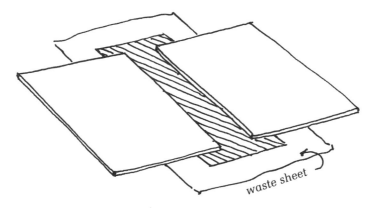

waste sheet

Center the inlay and turn in the cloth at head and tail, working it
down along the edges of the boards. Rub down both inlay and turn-ins
with a bone folder.

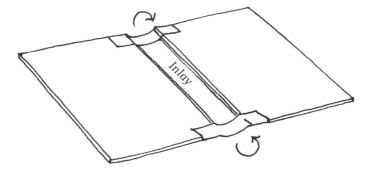

Inlay

If the original spine is still available, it can be centered on the newly made case. If not, a typed paper label can be used.

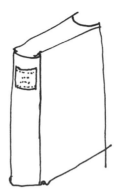

The bookblock can be attached to the case ("hung-in" is the bookbinding term) in the way described on pp. 138-142.

SHAKEN HINGES

This repair was invented by the conservator, Carolyn Horton, and is found in her book, Cleaning and Preserving Bindings and Related Materials. It is described here, using simpler equipment, with her permission.

Pastedowns and the extending spine lining often pull away from the boards without actually breaking.

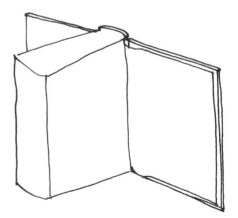

BOOKS: THEIR CARE AND REPAIR

A plastic bottle with a pointed cap is needed for this repair.

Cut the top of the cap with a pair of scissors so that the opening is slightly larger than a **medium-sized** knitting needle.

Put the needle all the way down in the bottle, which should be full of PVA. When you pull it out the cap will take most of the PVA off and leave the needle evenly coated with the right amount of adhesive.

Put the needle down into the hinge/joint area and hold the book tightly closed as you pull the needle out.

Repeat on the other side.

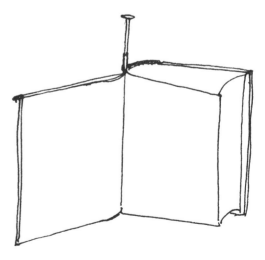

HINGE AND JOINT REPAIR

Work the cloth into the joints with a bone folder. Put a clean knitting needle in each joint (on the outside of the book, that is) and put it under boards and a heavy weight overnight.

You may find it easier to wrap the book in a bandage to hold the needles in place before putting a weight on it.

Wash the bottle cap thoroughly and put a layer or two of plastic wrap on the mouth of the bottle before putting the cap back on. This keeps the PVA from evaporating and saves the cap for future use.

Wash the knitting needles before the PVA has had time to dry.

BROKEN ADHESIVE BINDINGS

Adhesive bound books that have been bound with a poor adhesive often fall apart in sections.

This method of putting them back together may or may not work. It depends on the stiffness of the paper and the amount of old adhesive on the spine. However, it's worth a try.

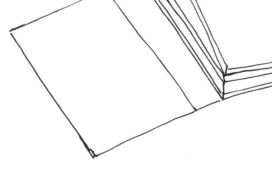

BOOKS: THEIR CARE AND REPAIR

Put a waste sheet about 1/16" in from
the spine edge of the bottom section.

Glue the exposed area.

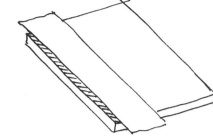

Position the next section on it so that
the head, tail, and spine edges are
lined up.

Repeat this process with all the sections
and then glue the whole spine.

Let the book dry for several hours under
a heavy weight or in a press, with
waxed paper and boards on either side.

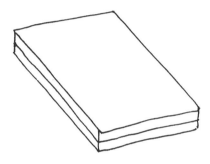

Glue the spine and put a paper
spine lining on it.

Let the lining extend about 1/16"
onto the front and back of the
textblock.

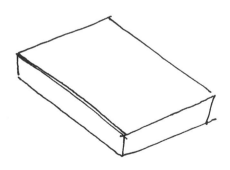

HINGE AND JOINT REPAIR

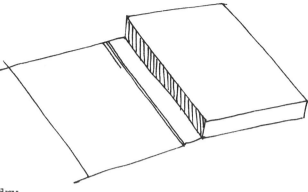

If the book has a soft cover,
glue the spine again and put
the cover back on. Rub it
tightly onto the spine with a
bone folder and let the book dry
overnight.

You need not put a weight on it.

If the book has a hard cover, you could make a new case with a flexible
spine using the original boards or make a new flexible cover out of
heavy paper.

Because there are so many variations in the way hinges and joints can
break, you may need to use a combination of the repairs described in
this chapter or work out some of your own.

These basic repairs can usually be done in under half an hour.

WRAPAROUNDS AND KYLE WRAPPERS

"Wraparounds" and "Kyle wrappers" are holding measures. They provide protection in cases where the cost of conservation would far exceed present value, but leave the door open for conservation in the future, when it may be warranted.

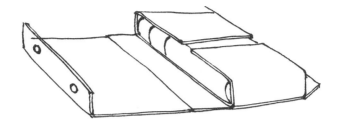

EQUIPMENT

The equipment and materials suggested in these lists are for books under 14" high. The amount of equipment listed is sufficient for one person.

Cutter or board shears }
Scoring machine   } Not absolutely necessary
Straight edge
Combination square
Utility knife or scalpel
Triangle
Bone folder
Scissors
Awl
Hole punch (optional)
Wooden applicator stick or a toothpick
Adhesive container

MATERIALS

The amounts given in parentheses are adequate for about 100 wraparounds or wrappers.

Thin, acid-free board, .040 or .050 for wraparounds (25-50 sheets)
Bristol board, 2- or 3-ply, or .020 acid-free board for Kyle wrappers
   (25-50 sheets)
Seine twine (1 ball)
Double-faced tape (4 rolls)
Buttons and pins (100-200)
PVA (1/4 cup)

The following techniques are largely specific to protective wrappers:

Adhering

Strong adhesion is needed if two pieces of
material are likely to pull away from each
other at a right angle to their surface.

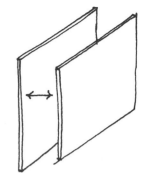

If the pull is parallel to the surface,
almost no adhesion is needed. This is
the case with wraparounds and Kyle
wrappers.

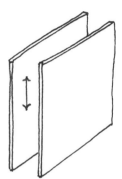

The inner and outer wrappers can be
held together with a few small
(about 1/16") dots of PVA or with
one or two strips of double-faced
tape.

SCORING AND FOLDING

The line where a bone folder scores
is not exactly at the edge along which
you are scoring, but half its own thickness away from that edge.

To score exactly on a mark, put the point
of the bone folder on it and bring the
edge against which you are scoring up
beside the bone folder.

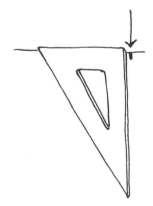

Score firmly, once for Bristol board,
at least three times for .040 or thicker board.

BOOKS: THEIR CARE AND REPAIR

Keep the scoring edge in place,
holding it down firmly, and bend
the board up at a slight angle
with the bone folder.

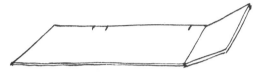

When all the folds in a board
have been scored and bent slightly,
bend each one all the way over.

The folds will follow the lines of
the scoring and initial bending.

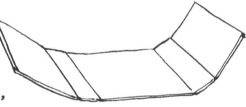

WRAPAROUNDS AND KYLE WRAPPERS

It is necessary to take the thickness of the board into account in measuring for a wraparound. Use the measuring unit BT (board thickness).

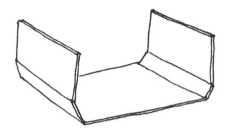

1 BT is taken up by the fold of thin board.

The thickness of the board used in wraparounds ranges from 1/32" to 1/16". Determine the thickness of the board you are using and use this measurement in adding or subtracting BT's. This can be done by eye.

Three measurements are needed for the inner wrapper: the height, width, and thickness of the book.

Height

Put a waste strip of paper
on the book and mark the height.

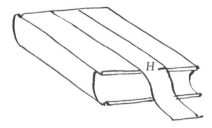

Width

The rounding of the spine must
be included in this measurement.
Put a triangle against the spine
of the book and measure from it
to the fore-edge.

BOOKS: THEIR CARE AND REPAIR

Thickness

Measure the thickness of the book with a combination square.

Transfer the measurement to the paper strip.

T *W* *H*

WRAPAROUNDS

They consist of two pieces of thin, acid-free board wrapped around the book at a right angle to each other, attached together and fastened at one edge.

Both the inner and outer parts of a wraparound should be cut from a board so that the grain of each is parallel to the folds.

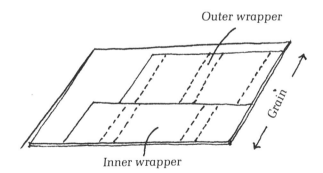

Outer wrapper

Grain

Inner wrapper

The dimension of the width of the
inner wrapper is the width of the
book plus 1/16".

Mark and cut the width.

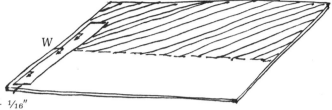

$+ \frac{1}{16}''$

W

Mark the position of the folds along
one edge of the strip of board,
adding or subtracting BT's by eye.

Cut the length of the wrapper.

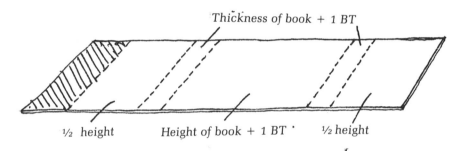

Thickness of book + 1 BT

½ height   Height of book + 1 BT   ½ height

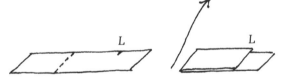

L   L

Fold the height measurement
marked on the strip of paper
in half to obtain this measurement.

Score and fold it.

164   BOOKS: THEIR CARE AND REPAIR

Outer wrapper

The inner wrapper with the book
in it is used to measure for the
outer wrapper.

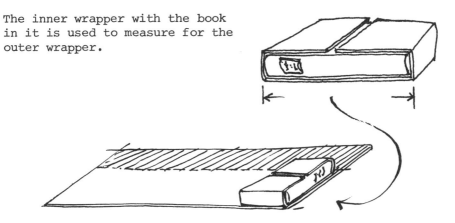

Mark and cut the height
of the outer wrapper.

Mark the folds of the wrapper:

Thickness less 1/8″

Width
plus 1 BT

*Thickness
plus 1 BT*

Width + 2 BTs

Thickness

Cut the width of the wrapper
and score and fold it as you
did the inner one.

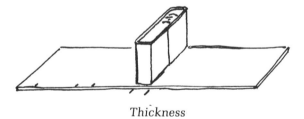

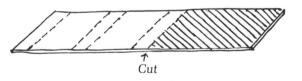

↑
Cut

BOOKS: THEIR CARE AND REPAIR

Punching holes in thin board is apt
to bend it.

A small, easily made jig supports the
board and prevents it from bending.

The jig can be made of strips of wood
such as lath or pieces of binder's
board glued or held together with
double-faced tape.

This jig can also be used as an
aid in scoring.

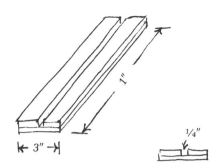

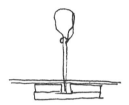

Mark the position of holes
for the ties and punch them,
using an awl, with the board
supported on the jig.

Punch from the outside in.

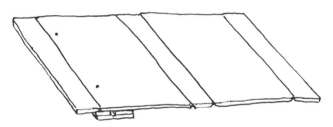

Lace a piece of twine
through the holes, leaving
about 3" extending.

Tie a single knot near each
end to keep the twine from
fraying.

WRAPAROUNDS AND KYLE WRAPPERS

Mark holes for the buttons corresponding to the position of the twine and approximately centered on the length of the small flap.

Punch two holes for each button, supporting the board with the jig.

The holes should be about 1/16" apart.

Move the awl back and forth between the two holes to form an oval one that will fit the shaft of the button.

An alternative method is to use a hole punch that punches ovals or small triangles.

Two triangles punched side by side make a neat hole for the button. ▲▲

BOOKS: THEIR CARE AND REPAIR

Put the shank of the button in
the hole while the board is still
on the jig.

Slide the pin through the shank
of the button.

If you are using thin board the pin may be loose. If so, glue a small
square of cloth over the pin so that it won't slip out of the button
shank.

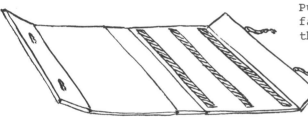

Put down 3 strips of double-
faced tape, slightly in from
the edges and folds.

Remove the brown paper from the tape and position the inner wrapper.
Press down firmly.

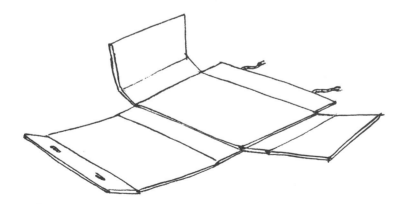

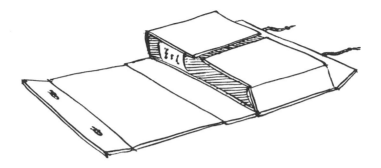

With practice -- and a cutter -- a wraparound can be made in fifteen minutes.

KYLE WRAPPERS

This ingenious protective cover was designed by Hedi Kyle, head conservator at the Book Preservation Center of the New York Botanical Garden, and is described here with her permission.

Like wraparounds, these wrappers consist of two pieces of thin board wrapped around the book at a right angle to each other and attached together.

Measure the height, width, and thickness of the book and mark the measurements on a paper strip. See pp. 162-163.

Inner wrapper

Cut a rectangle (pp. 160-161) of 2- or 3- ply Bristol board or .020 acid-free board the height of the book by 2-1/2 times the width plus 3 times the thickness less 2 BT's at one end.

Cut off these corners. This can be done with scissors or with a scalpel.

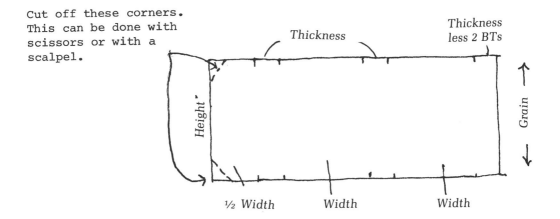

Score with a triangle or mark the dimensions on the opposite edge and score and bend as described on pp. 160-161.

Marking both edges is usually a more accurate method than using the triangle.

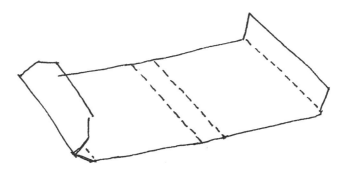

Outer wrapper

Cut another Bristol board rectangle the width of the book by twice the height plus 2 BT's plus twice the thickness.

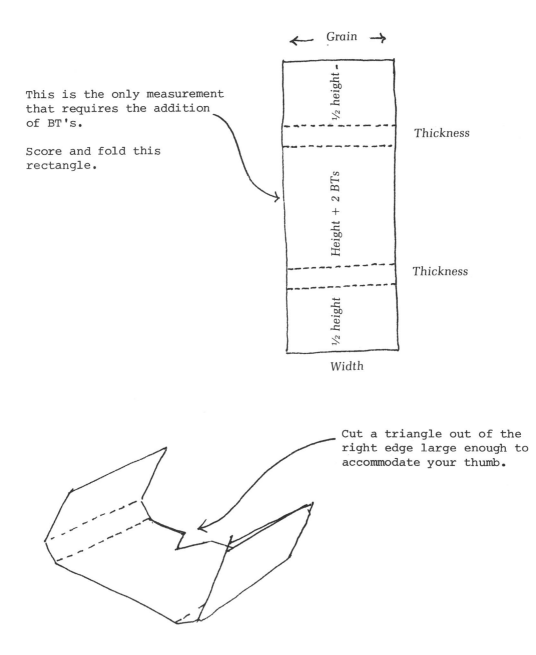

← Grain →

½ height

Thickness

Height + 2 BTs

Thickness

½ height

Width

This is the only measurement that requires the addition of BT's.

Score and fold this rectangle.

Cut a triangle out of the right edge large enough to accommodate your thumb.

BOOKS: THEIR CARE AND REPAIR

The two folded pieces of Bristol board are very much like those of a wraparound.

The difference is in the way they go together and close.

Put 3 or more dots of PVA or a strip of double-faced tape about 3/4" in from the left edge of the outer wrapper.

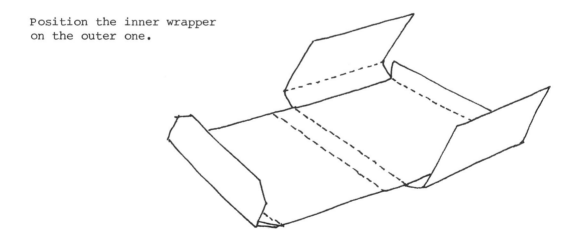

Position the inner wrapper on the outer one.

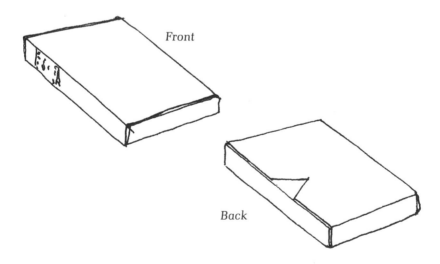

Close flaps A and B and
bring flap C around and in
between the inner and outer
wrappers underneath the book.

Asterisks or other symbols can be
used on a typed label both for
decoration and for cutting guides.

```
***************************
        Homer
        ILIAD
***************************
```

The wrapper is held shut without additional fastening.

Front

Back

BOOKS: THEIR CARE AND REPAIR

EXHIBITION TECHNIQUES

All library materials are damaged by light. Heat and excesses of relative humidity are also damaging and frequently occur in exhibition cases. Books should not be held open in one place for any length of time -- four months should be the maximum time for exhibition and two months is preferable.

The best conditions for the exhibition materials are:

1. The lowest adequate light level -- and one which excludes ultraviolet radiation.

2. The lowest temperature possible and a stable relative humidity of between 40 and 60%.

3. Adequate support for the material.

Specific steps that can be taken to control or improve the climate in exhibition cases and areas are to:

Curtain windows
Paint over skylights
Put ultraviolet filtering sleeves on fluorescent lights
Have the light source outside exhibition cases, particularly
    if the light is incandescent as it generates a lot of heat
Turn off some of the lights in the cases. It is often pos-
    sible to cut the light level in half without having it
    noticed.

ENVIRONMENT

Simple monitoring devices can give you guidelines for improvements in the exhibit environment and also show the public, trustees, or possible donors, that you are concerned about the materials in your care.

Light

Blue wool samples (See p. 50) monitor light. They are inexpensive little cards with strips of blue wool cloth pasted on them. The cloth of each strip fades at a different rate.

Tape the card to a stiff piece of cardboard and tape a strip of black paper or other opaque material on top of it with double-faced tape.

The cardboard holds the blue wool card rigid so that light will not seep under the opaque shield.

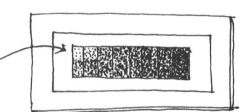

There is a very complicated method for calculating the rate of fading, but I have found that being able to demonstrate that fading is taking place is enough to generate action -- the installation of a curtain or the removal of the object from exhibition, for example.

Check the card at one-week intervals.

Write on the back of the card the date you put it in position.

Position the card facing the light source in an exhibition case or on a wall.

Check the card at one-week intervals. You will be surprised at how quickly evidence of fading shows up.

Heat and Humidity

Cheap temperature/relative humidity monitors are readily available and are adequate unless you really require scientific accuracy.

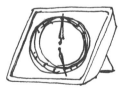

EQUIPMENT

Cutter or board shears
Bone folder
Scalpel and/or mat knife
1" oil painting brush
Straight edge
Triangle
Blocks or other supports
Adhesive container

MATERIALS

Board
    Binder's board, .98 or heavier (1 board)
    Acid-free board, .040 or .050 (3 sheets)
    Mat board, 2- or 4-ply (2 sheets)
    Polyester film, .002 (3 yds.)
    Double-faced tape (1 roll)
    Kizukishi (1 sheet)
    Cornstarch paste
    Newsprint

The amounts in parentheses are enough for a start. It's impossible
to guess how you want to display what materials.

HOLDING BOOKS OPEN

Books can be held open with 1/2" to 1-1/2" wide strips of polyester
film, the width depending on the size of the book.

The length should be more than twice the height of the book.

Put a piece of double-faced tape about 2/3 the height of the book down on one end of the polyester film strip.

Wrap the strip snugly around the book using the double-faced tape to adhere the ends of the film strip together.

There should be a long overlap.

If the edges of the pages are very fragile, cut 2 pieces of polyester film 2" or 3" wide by the thickness of the part of the book that you are holding opened plus 2".

Wrap these strips around the head and tail of the book and wrap the taped strip around on top of them.

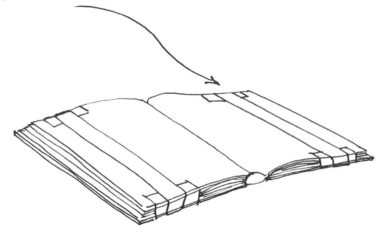

SUPPORTS AND CRADLES

Supports should be made of attractive but neutral colored materials. Their design varies depending on whether the book is to be displayed standing up, lying down, or slanting, and opened near the front, back, or center.

178   BOOKS: THEIR CARE AND REPAIR

There are various supports for books lying down:

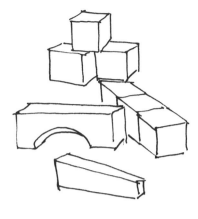

Children's unpainted blocks,
which come in a variety of sizes;

Pieces of 2" x 4" lumber, which can
be of various lengths or cut at
an angle to make wedges;

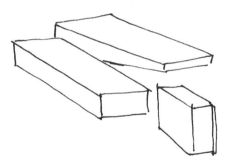

Piles of binder's or other board,
which can be used to bring blocks
of 2" x 4"s to the correct height,
or in a pile by themselves.

If the book is opened near
the front or back, support
the board and adjacent leaves
so that they are level with the
plane of the text.

If the book is to be open
in the center, use wedge-
shaped supports.

A cradle can also be made
for books displayed lying
down.

Measure the outside of the
book when it is held open
less about 2" with a strip
of paper.

Open the book only as far as
it will go without undue
strain.

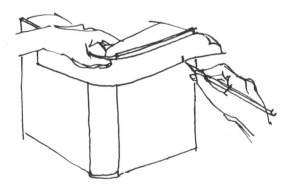

BOOKS: THEIR CARE AND REPAIR

Cut a piece of .040 or .050 board to a width of about 2" less than the height of the book and mark the center of the long edge.

Fold your measurement from the outside of the book in half and mark it, centered, on the board.

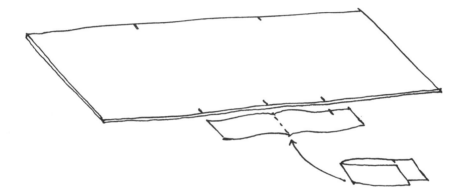

Mark the dimensions of the uprights. They should be between 2-3/4" and 4" high, depending on how wide you want the book to open.

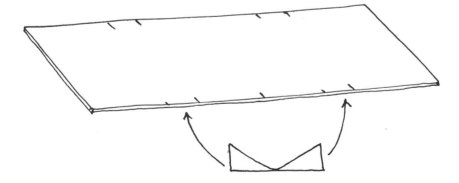

EXHIBITION TECHNIQUES

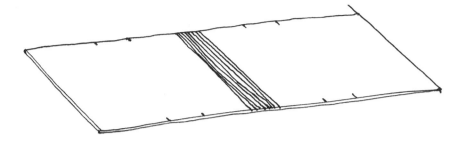

Cut lines about 1/8" apart for about 2-1/2" at the center. Cut lightly with a scalpel and straight edge, cutting less than halfway through the board. This allows the cradle to adjust to the spine of many books instead of to just one.

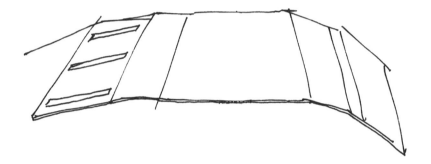

Score along the marks with a bone folder and fold the board. Put 3 strips of double-faced tape down on the outside of one of the base flaps.

Fold the board around like this and attach the base flaps together so that the uprights are at a right angle to the base.

　　　　　　　　　　BOOKS: THEIR CARE AND REPAIR

The weight of the book will make
the uprights slant in slightly.

If the book is open in the center,
the cradle will probably stay upright, but it is best to tape the
center of the cradle in position
or wedge the cradle upright with
a small weight.

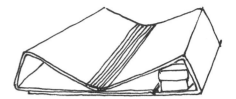

You can change the angle of the
cradle. In this case, taping or
wedging is absolutely necessary

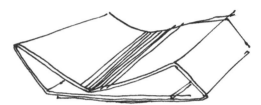

If a book is inclined to close, the base of the cradle can be taped to a
piece of stiff material such as binder's board or masonite.

The book can then be attached to the cradle and base with polyester
strips.

The polyester strips must be
attached around the supporting
board only, not around the base.

Fasten the strips with double-
faced tape and then slide the
fastenings around to the inside
of the cradle so that they don't
show.

EXHIBITION TECHNIQUES

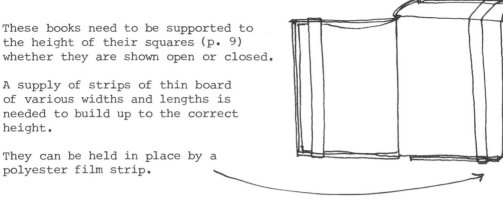

These books need to be supported to
the height of their squares (p. 9)
whether they are shown open or closed.

A supply of strips of thin board
of various widths and lengths is
needed to build up to the correct
height.

They can be held in place by a
polyester film strip.

If the board you use is not attractive in
itself, it can be wrapped in a piece of
paper or cloth that is.

Do not display books upright unless they are still firmly bound.

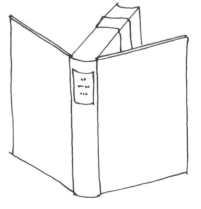

If you are displaying a book
this way, tape the textblock
together and support it as
described above.

BOOKS: THEIR CARE AND REPAIR

BOOKS DISPLAYED SLANTING

A very simple cradle can be made to exhibit books at a slant. One size of cradle can be used to support many sizes of book.

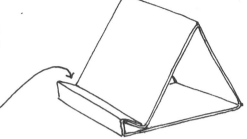

Only the slanted surface against which the book rests need relate to the size of the book. It should be slightly shorter and narrower than the book it will display.

This angle should be a right angle.

Here are specific measurements for a cradle for use with books ranging in dimension from about 6" x 9" to about 8" x 10".

Cut a piece of .040 or .050 board 5" wide by 26-1/2" long, grain short. Mark and score it for folding.

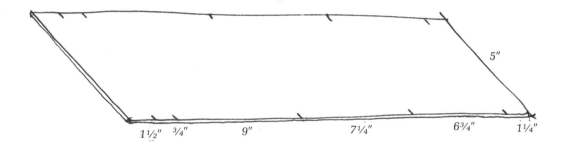

5"

1½" ¾"   9"   7¼"   6¾"   1¼"

All the scoring and folding can be done on one side of the board except this fold, which needs to be reversed after the initial folding.

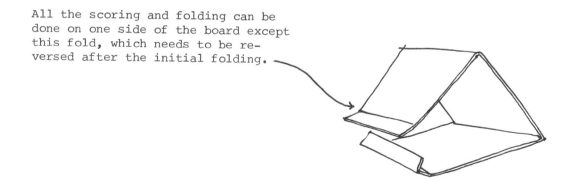

Put two strips of double-faced
tape down on this end flap.

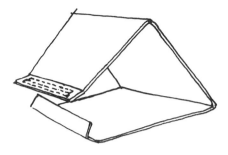

Tape the two end flaps together.

The cradle will look like this.

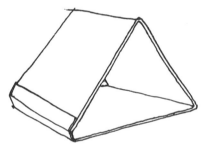

The weight of the book will make
it look like this.

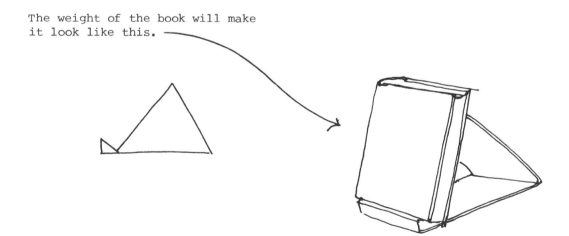

BOOKS: THEIR CARE AND REPAIR

If the book is thicker than the shelf's width, cut a piece of board the thickness of the book by its width and put it on the shelf under the book.

Support the bookblock to the height of the squares with thin pieces of board (p. 184).

For a book displayed open, double the width of the cradle.

Do not leave out the supports under the bookblock as was done in the drawing.

For a large book, the following dimensions for the piece of board for the cradle work well: 7" or 8" wide by 34" long, grain short. If you can't have a piece of board that long, you can hinge smaller pieces together at one or more of the folds。

If the book is very heavy, the back support will bow out and you may need to put a piece of stiff board (heavy binder's board or masonite) inside the triangle. It need not be attached.

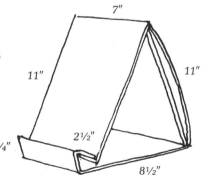

Documents present no problems unless the temperature inside the exhibition case causes them to curl. To prevent this, put the document on a piece of thin board and then to hold it flat use strips of polyester film attached behind the board with double-faced tape.

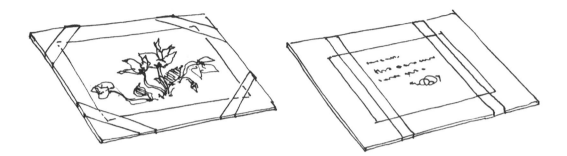

Documents displayed vertically

Obviously, documents displayed vertically must be attached to something.

They can be mounted on a support board with a window mat, in which case two mats or other thin boards the same size are needed.

A window or windows can be cut in one board and the document hinged to the other, which is the support board.

Draw the window on the back of the board, being sure that it is square with the edge. It should be about 1/4" to 1/2" smaller than the document in each direction.

Cut it out with a utility knife or scalpel and a straight edge.

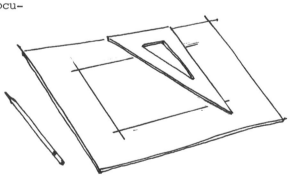

BOOKS: THEIR CARE AND REPAIR

If you need several windows in one window
board that look like this,

 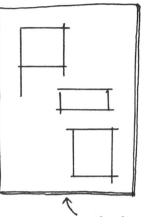

remember to draw the guidelines for cutting in reverse on the back of
the board. Draw on the back of the window board in order to keep the
front absolutely clean.

After making a window, line
up the two pieces of board and
make a small pencil mark in the
corners of the window on the
support board.

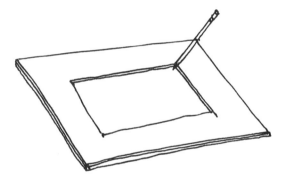

Center one edge of the document
with the corresponding window
corner marks and mark the board
where the corners of the document come to.

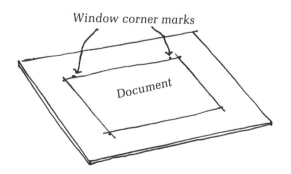

Window corner marks

Document

Draw lines through the outer pair of marks on each side.

This gives you the position of the document in relation to the window.

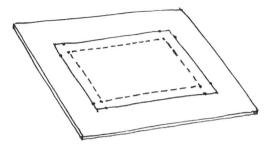

Depending on the size of the document, cut 2, 3, or 4 rectangles of Japanese tissue about 1" x 2", to serve as hinges. Kizukishi is a good weight to use。

Make a fairly stiff cornstarch paste. (Cook it a little longer than usual.)

Fold the hinges 1/2" from the end.

Paste the 1/2" section.

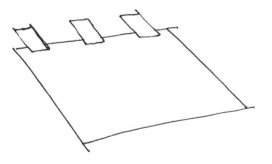

Position the hinges, more or less evenly spaced, on the back of the document.

Rub them down with a bone folder. Put a piece of waxed paper and a weight on them, and let them dry for an hour or two.

If you are in a hurry and have a hair dryer, you can dry them with that.

BOOKS: THEIR CARE AND REPAIR

Position the document
and put a weight on it
to hold it in place.

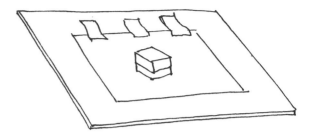

Fold the extending portion of
the hinges back with a waste
strip under them, and paste
and put them down on the
board.

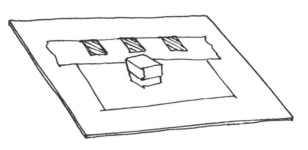

Remove the waste sheet, rub
down with a bone folder, and
let the hinges dry overnight
under waxed paper and a weight.

The support board and the window board can be held together with double-
faced tape or hinged together at the top with a strip of bookcloth about
1-1/2" wide.

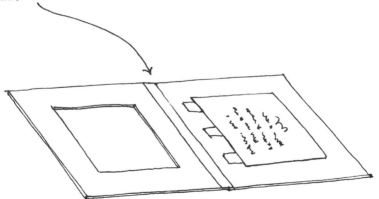

Position the two boards right beside each other and put weights on them to hold them in place.

Mark 1/2" in from the top on two sides of one of the boards.

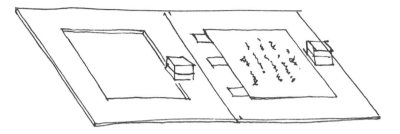

Glue the hinge on a waste sheet and put it down, lining it up with the 1/2" marks. Rub it down well.

Documents can be matted with 1/8" to 1/4" of each edge covered by the window board, as just described, or they can be matted with the entire document showing.

In the latter case they need to be hinged so that the hinge will not show.

Cut a window about 1/4" to 1/2" larger than the document on all four sides. Save the cut out piece to use later (p. 195).

Mark the corners of the window on the support board and place the document where you want it in relation to these marks.

Mark the top corners of the document on the supporting board and position the document, lined up with the marks and upside down.

Put a weight on it.

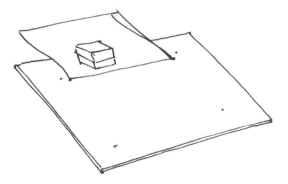

Cut 2 or 3 rectangles of
Japanese tissue about
1" x 2-1/2".

Paste each hinge all over and put
it down with about 1/2" on the
document and the remaining 2"
on the board.

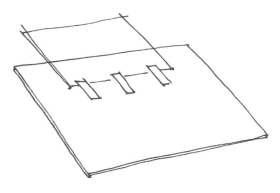

Cut 2 or 3 strips of Japanese tissue
about 1/2" x 2".

Paste each one and put it across
each hinge like this.

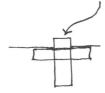

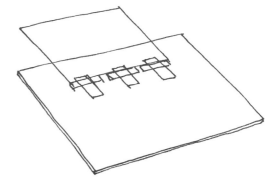

This prevents the weight of the
document from pulling the hinge
away from the board.

Put a piece of waxed paper on the
hinges, just below the top edge
of the document, and fold the
document over.

It is possible to make some
adjustment at this point. Be
sure the document lines up
correctly in relation to the
window.

EXHIBITION TECHNIQUES

Put a piece of waxed paper on top of the **document. Put the window cut-**out back in place and let the hinges dry under a board and a weight overnight.

Hinge or tape the mounting boards together.

Documents mounted on a board without a window can also be held in place with a T hinge.

When the exhibition is over the document can be cut off the mount at the fold of the hinge and the tissue wet with a damp cotton swab.

Let the moisture soak in for a few minutes until the tissue is ready to lift off in one piece. The remaining cornstarch paste can be wiped off with the cotton swab when any excess water has been squeezed out of it.

Let the damp areas dry under waxed paper (in case there is still a slight residue of adhesive) and a weight.

Small documents can be held in place by strips of polyester film laced through slits in a board at the corners of the document and taped on the back.

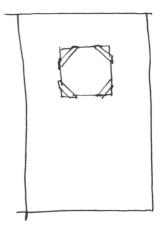

Back of board

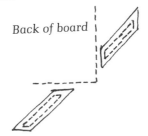

Small documents can also be encapsulated (pp. 84-90) and the envelope pinned to the upright surface. Clear, colorless push pins are not very noticeable against polyester film.

Small triangular supports for labels can be made from board scraps.
They are put together in the same way as the book cradles.

BIBLIOGRAPHY

The Abbey Newsletter: Bookbinding and Conservation.

> This publication lists sales of binding equipment and supplies and gives information on testing of materials and other activities in the conservation/preservation field. It can be ordered from the following address: c/o School of Library Service, 516 Butler Library, Columbia University, New York, New York 10027.

Baynes-Cope, A. D. Caring for Books and Documents. London: Published for the Trustees of the British Museum by British Museum Publications Ltd., 1981.

> A short book on the proper storage and handling of books.

Cunha, George Martin and Grant, Dorothy. Conservation of Library Materials: A Manual and Bibliography on the Care, Repair and Restoration of Library Materials. 2nd ed. Metuchen, N.J.: The Scarecrow Press, Inc., 1971. 2 vols.

> Volume I contains the historical background of the book and information on preventive care, repair, and restoration, and disaster planning. Volume II is a comprehensive bibliography.

DeCandido, Robert. "Preserving our Library Materials." Library Scene, September-December 1978, pp. 10-12; March 1979, pp. 4-6; June 1979, pp. 4,5; September 1979, pp. 6-8.

> These articles cover the nature of paper and paper deterioration; preservation treatments available to librarians; environmental factors affecting library materials, and emergencies in libraries.

Greenfield, Jane and Walker, Gay. Flood: Immediate Action Manual. New Haven: Yale University Library, 1983. Available from Preservation Department, Yale University Library, New Haven, CT 06520.

> Although this was written specifically for the use of the Yale libraries, the procedures outlined can be adapted for use in any library.

Horton, Carolyn. Cleaning and Preserving Bindings and Related Materials. 2nd ed. rev. Chicago: American Library Association, Library Technology Program, 1969.

> A very complete book on this subject. A third edition will be published soon.

Kyle, Hedi et al. Library Materials Preservation Manual. Bronxville, N.Y.: Nicholas T. Smith, 1983.

Available from the publisher, Box 66, Bronxville, NY 10708.

Step-by-step techniques for in-house repair.

Library of Congress Preservation Leaflets. <u>Selected References in the Literature of Conservation</u>. <u>Environmental Protection of Books and Related Materials</u>. <u>Preserving Leather Bookbindings</u>. <u>Marking Manuscripts</u>. <u>Preserving Newspapers and Newspaper-Type Materials</u>, 1975-1977.

A brief introduction to these subjects.

Available, free of charge, from the Library of Congress, Attn: Assistant Director for Preservation, Administrative Department, Washington, DC 20540.

Morrow, Carolyn Clark. <u>Conservation Treatment Procedures: A Manual of Step-by-Step Procedures for the Maintenance and Repair of Library Materials</u>. Littleton, Colorado: Libraries Unlimited, Inc., 1982.

A basic how-to text.

Roberts, Matt T. and Etherington, Don. <u>Bookbinding and the Conservation of Books: A Dictionary of Descriptive Terminology</u>. Washington: Library of Congress, 1982.

A glossary of preservation, conservation, and bookbinding terms.

Swartzburg, Susan G. <u>Preserving Library Materials: A Manual</u>. Metuchen, N.J. and London: The Scarecrow Press, Inc., 1980.

A guide to help librarians analyze their needs.

Waters, Peter. <u>Procedures for Salvage of Water-Damaged Materials</u>. Washington: Library of Congress, 1975.

A detailed treatment of this subject.

Young, Laura S. <u>Bookbinding & Conservation by Hand: A Working Guide</u>. New York and London: R. R. Bowker Company, 1981.

A book on fine binding and conservation techniques for rare materials.

Audio-visual materials: Three slide/tape shows are available from the Preservation Department, Yale University Library, New Haven, CT 06520.

They were prepared by NEH/Mellon Grant interns at Yale under the direction and editorship of Jane Greenfield and Gay Walker. They are: "The Care and Handling of Books," "Commercial Library Binding: The Librarian's View," and "Simple Repairs for Library Materials." Many of the repairs described in this book are shown in the latter.

INDEX

Ace bandage, 50
Acid migration, preventing, 82
Acid-free board, 51
  for wraparounds, 163
  in making Kyle wrappers, 171-74
  mat board, 53
Acid-free paper, 50
  in storing paper documents, 82
  Permalife paper, 53
  wrapping fragile material in, 104
Adhesion, 160
Adhesives, 31-32
  see also Pastes; Pasting
  containers for, 42
Adhesive-bound books, 12
  repair of, 156-58
Adhesive-bound pamphlets, 109,
  123-26
Air pollution, book deterioration
  and, 20
Aluminum-post binding, 13
Applicator sticks, 50
  see also Cotton swabs
Aqueous deacidification, 83
Archival materials
  handling, 82
  storage containers for, 54, 82
Awl, 42
  in making wraparounds, 167, 168
  in pamphlet binding, 114, 119-20

Barrier board, 50
Beeswax, 50
Bending paper or board, to determine grain direction, 24
Binders, ring and spiral, 14
Binder's board, 50
  in displaying books, 179
  in encapsulation, 84
Binding pamphlets, see Pamphlet
  binding
Bindings
  adhesive, 12, 156-58
  see also Adhesive-bound
    pamphlets
  case binding, 19
  oriental, 14
  sewn or stapled, 13
  pamplets, 110, 123-26
  wooden board, 15th century, 19
Blotting paper, 50
Blue prints, flattening, 67
Blue wool samples, 50
  for monitoring fading of exhibi-
    tion materials, 175-76
Board
  barrier, 50
  binder's, 50, 84, 179
  Bristol, see Bristol board
  cardboard, see Cardboard

for cutting, 28-29, 55
for displaying books, 179, 181-83,
  185
for displaying documents, 188-94
for pressing, 40
grain direction of, determining,
  25
in flattening paper, 66
in making pamphlet covers, 112
  adhesive-bound, 123-26
  multiple-signature, 121-22
  single-signature, 115-17
in making wraparounds, see
  Wraparounds
lig-free, 52
masonite, 84
mat, 53
measuring, 27
pasting, 30
scoring, 41
storage of, 49
Board shears and cutters, 36-38
Board thickness (BT), 27
  in measuring for pamphlet cov-
    ers, 112
Bone folder, 42
  in making book pockets, 105
  in making pamphlet covers, 116,
    117, 118
  in mending overlapping tears, 76
  in repairing broken hinges, 137
  in scoring and folding wrapa-
    rounds, 160-61
  in spine repair, 150
  in tipping-in, 94, 95, 97-99
Bookbinding, requirements for, 12
Bookblock, 17
  case and, attachment between,
    130-31
  pulled away from case, repair of,
    140-42
  stapled, 110
Book pages
  mending, 68
  see also Paper treatment
  tipping-in, see Tipping-in
Bookplating, 89-90
Book pockets, 104-7
Book repair
  see also specific headings e.g.
    Mending, Pasting, etc.
  materials suppliers, 55-59
Books
  deterioration of, 20-21
  displaying, see Exhibition mate-
    rials
  dusting and cleaning, 21
  hinge and joint repair, see Hinge
    and joint repair
  parts of a book, 11
  shelving, 21

Bookworms, treatment of, 21
Bottles, plastic, with pointed tip,
  44, 155, 156
  in hinge and joint repair, 155,
    156
Brick weights, making, 46-48
Bristol board, 50-51
  acid-free, 51
  for making pockets for fragile
    material, 126-28
  grain of, 24, 126
  in making book pockets, 104-7
  in making Kyle wrappers, 171-74
Brushes
  for cleaning, 43
  for pasting, 32-33, 43, 75
  in dry cleaning paper, 62, 63
BT see Board thickness
Buckram, 50
Buttons, 51
  in making wraparounds, 169

Cardboard
  as cutting surface, 55
  in tipping-in, 103
  use of, 28
Case binding, 19
Casemaker, 41
Casing in, 19
  see also Hinge and joint repair
Chain lines, 23
Chain stitch, for sewing signatures,
  16
Chair, for book repair work, 36
Charcoal drawings, treatment of, 83
Charcoal paper, 51
Children's blocks, for displaying
  books, 179
Cleaning books, 21
  see also Dry cleaning
Cloth
  buckram, 50
  in repairing detached spine, 143-
    46
  lawn cloth, 52
  mull, 53
  muslin, 53
  Oxford, 50
  Super, 54, 130
  thread direction, determining,
    26
Cockroaches, treatment of, 21
Codex format, 12
Combination press, 39-40
Combination square, 44
  in measuring wraparounds, 163
Containers
  for adhesives, 42
  plastic bottle with pointed tip,
    44, 155, 156
  for storage, 54

Cord, 51
  see also String and twine
  (for sewing pamphlets, 125
Cornstarch, 51
Cornstarch paste, 31-32
Cotton swabs, Q Tips, 53
Cradles, for displaying books, 178-83
Cutting, 28-29
  see also Shears and cutters
  carboard for, 55
  masonite for, 55
  mending strips, 70

Deacidification
  for encapsulation, 83
  solution for, 51
Documents
  see also Encapsulation; Paper treatment
  displaying, 188-94
  matting, 192-94
Double-faced tape, 51
  encapsulating with, 83-87
  in holding books open for display, 178, 183
  in making book display supports, 186
  in making book pockets, 106-7
  in making wraparounds, 169
Drawings, treatment of, 83
Drilling holes, for sewing pamphlets, 125
Drills, electric, 44
Drill press, 41
Dry cleaning, 62-64
  materials for, 61
Drying, table for, 42
Dustcloths, 51-52
  in encapsulation, 85-88
Dusting books, 21

Electric drill, 44
Elmer's glue, 31
Encapsulation, 83-89
  materials for, 62
  mending for, 68-72
  of small documents, 194
  with double-faced tape, 83-87
Endsheets, 17, 130
Erasers
  gum, 52
  in dry cleaning paper, 64
  kneaded, 52
  Magic Rub, 52
  Pink Pearl eraser, 64
Exhibition materials, displaying, 175-95
  books at a slant, 185-87
  books in upright position, 184
  documents, 188-94
  environmental conditions for, 175-76
  open books, 177-78
  supports and cradles for, 178-83

Fading
  causes of, 20
  monitoring rate of, 175-76
Flattening, 64-67
  bookplates, 89
  materials for, 61
  table for, 42
Flyleaves, repair of, 136
Folded documents, flattening, 67
Folded sheets
  endsheets, 17
  tipping-in, 101-2
  signatures, see Signatures
Folding
  board for book display, 182, 185
  Kyle wrappers, 171-74
  wraparounds, 160-61
Folio, 15

Gampi, thin, 52
Gatherings see Signatures
Glues, gluing see Adhesive headings; Pastes; Pasting
Grain, 22
  chain lines and, 23
  direction of, determining, 23-26
  of board, 25
  Bristol board, 126
  for wraparounds, 163
  of mending strips, 70
  of paper, 23-25
  of waste paper strips, 55
Graph paper, 52
  in encapsulation, 84
Guarding, 98-100
Gum erasers, 52
  in dry cleaning paper, 64

Handling
  books, 21
  paper, 82
Handling suports, making, 82
  materials for, 62
Headbands, replacing, 135
Heat
  book deterioration and, 20
  exhibition materials and, 175
Hinge and joint repair, 129-58
  broken adhesive bindings, 156-58
  broken hinges and joints, 134-40, 151-54
  case and bookblock pulled apart, 140-42
  equipment and materials for, 131-33
  flapping spine with boards attached, 142-50
  reinforcing cloth hinges, 133
  shaken hinges, 154-56
Hinges
  for document display, 190-93
  of books, see Hinge and joint repair
  t-hinge, 193
Holepunch, 44
  in making wraparounds, 168

Holes
  in paper, see Lacunae
  drilling, for sewing pamphlets, 125
Humidifiers, 41
Humidifying
  paper, 64, 65
  exhibition materials, 175, 176
Humidity monitors, 176
Humidity, book deterioration and, 20

Ink solubility, testing for, 67

Japanese tissue, 52
  see also Mending strips
  in making document display hinges, 190-92, 193
  in reinforcing flyleaves, 136
  in reinforcing cloth hinges, 133
  in repairing lacunae, 72, 80-81
  in tipping-in, 96-97, 98-100, 101
Jig, in making wraparounds, 167, 168
Joint repair, see Hinge and joint repair

Kizukishi, 52
  for making document display hinges, 190
Kneaded erasers, 52
  in dry cleaning paper, 64
Knitting needles, in hinge and joint repair, 155-56
Knife
  see also Scalpel; Utility knife
  in removing staples, 44, 113
  use of, for cutting, 28
Kyle wrappers, 170-74
  equipment and materials for, 159

Labels, for exhibition materials, 195
Lacunae, repairing
  in documents to be encapsulated, 68
  patches for, 71-72, 80-81
Lawn cloth, 52
Letter press, 38-39, 132
Light, book deterioration and, 20, 175-76
Lighting, for book repair work, 36
Light monitors, 175-76
Lig-free board, 52
Linen thread, 54
Lying press, 132

Magic Rub eraser, 52
  in dry cleaning paper, 64
Maps, covers for, 126-28
Masking tape, 52
Masonite
  as cutting surface, 55
  in encapsulation, 84
Matting documents, 192-94
Mat board, 53
Measuring, 26-27

combination square for, 44
for tipping-in, 93-94
newsprint strips for, 143, 144
pamphlet covers, 112
wraparounds, 162-63
Mending, 67-72
see also Pasting
materials for, 61-62
supports for, 69-70
Mending strips, 70-71
for reinforcing tears, 76-77
pasting, 72-74
tearing, 71
Methyl cellulose, 53
in making paste, 32
Microspatula, 44
in reinforcing tears, 78
Mull, 53, 130
Muslin, 53
Mylar film, 53
see also Polyester film

Needles, 44
knitting, 155-56
potter's cut-off, 45, 114, 119-20
Newsprint, 53, 54
in flattening paper, 65-67
strips of, for measuring, 143, 144
Nipping press, 38-39, 132

Oil painting brushes, 43
storing, 33
Opaline pads, 53
in dry cleaning paper, 63
Overlapping tears, repairing, 74-77
Oversewn binding, 13
Oxford cloth, 51

Pamphlet binding, 108-28
adhesive-bound or side-stapled,
109, 110, 123-26
equipment and materials for,
110-11
measuring for, 112
multiple-signature, 108-9, 118-23
single-signature, 108, 113-18
Paper
see also Paper treatment
acid-free, *see* Acid-free paper
blotting, 50
charcoal, 51
cutting, 28-29
encapsulation of, *see* Encapsulation
grain of, 22-25
graph, 52
Japanese tissue, *see* Japanese tissue
newsprint, *see* Newsprint
Permalife, 53, 104
sandpaper, 53
Strathmore 400, 54
waxed, *see* Waxed paper
Paperbacks, 12
Paper strips, measuring with, 27

Paper treatment, 60-89
dry cleaning, 62-64
encapsulation *see* Encapsulation
equipment and materials, 61-62
flattening, 64-67
humidifying, 41, 64, 65
handling, 82
mending, 67-72
pasting, 30, 72-81
storage, 49, 62, 82
Paring knife, for removing staples,
44
Pastel drawings, treatment of, 83
Pastes, 31-32
containers for, 42
wheat, 55
Pasting, 30, 72-81
adhesion, 160
adhesive-bound books, 157
bookplates, 89-90
edge tears, 72-73
filling in lacunae, 80-81
in hinge and joint repair, 136,
139, 141
overlapping tears, 74-77
pamphlet covers, 116, 117, 122,
124
plate glass as surface for, 44
shaken hinges, 155-56
spine inlay, 145
tears with no overlap, 77-79
tip-ins, 94
Pasting brushes, care of, 32-33
Pasting sheets, 54
Patches, for repairing lacunae, 71-
72, 80-81
Penn-made linen cord, 51
Permalife paper, 53, 104
Photocopies
flattening, 67
for tipping-in, 97
Photographs, flattening, 67
Pink Pearl eraser, 64
Plastic bottle with pointed tip, 44
in hinge and joint repair, 155,
156
Plate glass
as pasting surface, 44
as mending surface, 73
Pockets
for books, 104-7
for fragile material, 126-28
Polyester film, 53
in bookplating, 90
in displaying documents, 188,
194
in encapsulation, 84-88
in holding books open for display, 177-78, 183-84
in repairing lacunae, 71-72
sewing, by machine, 87
Polyester web, 45
in flattening paper, 65-67
Polyvinyl acetate emulsion, *see*
PVA
Potter's cut-off needle, 45
in pamplet binding, 114, 119-20

Presses, 38-41
for hinge and joint repair, 132,
137, 140
Pressing paper, 65-66
Pressing boards, 40
Pressure-sensitive tape, mending
with, 21
PVA, 31, 53
"50/50" mixture, 32
in making Kyle wrappers, 173
in repairing shaken hinges, 155-
56

Quarto, 15

Rare materials
handling, 82
treatment of, 60
Ring binders, 14
Rolled documents, flattening, 66
Rug shears, 29, 45

Sable brushes, 43
care of, 33
Sanding spine linings, 135
Sandpaper, 53
Scalpel, 28, 45
in cutting mending strips, 70
in making cradles for book display, 182
in repairing broken hinges, 134
in spine repair, 147
in tipping-in, 96, 103
Scissors, *see* Shears and cutters
Scoring
board for book display, 182, 185
Kyle wrappers, 171-74
wraparounds, 160-61
Scoring machine, 41
Seine twine, 54
Sewing
encapsulating documents by, 87-
89
pamphlets:
adhesive-bound, 125-26
multiple-signature, 119-20
single-signature, 114
signatures, 16-17
tip-ins, 101-2
Sewing machine, 42
in sewing polyester film, 87
Sewn bindings, 13
Oriental, 14
Shears and cutters
for board, 36-38
old model Jacques, 37
rug shears, 29, 45
Shelving books, 21
Side-stapled pamphlets, 110, 123-
26
Signatures, 15-16
sewing, 16-17
Silk tissue, 52
Silverfish, treatment of, 21
Sink, for book repair work, 36

Sobo bottle, 44
Spine, 17-18
Spine inlay, 145-46
  original, removing, 146-47
Spine lining, 18, 134-39
Spine repair
  adhesive-bound books, 157-58
  detached spine, 142-50
  spine lining, 134-39
Spiral binders, 14
Spots, on paper, removing, 64
Stabbed bindings, 13
  Oriental, 14
Stapled bindings, 13
  pamphlets, 110, 123-26
Staples, 54
  removing from pamphlet bind-
    ings, 113
Stapling, in encapsulation, 88, 89
Stiff bristle brushes, 33
Stool, for book repair work, 36
Storage
  containers for, 54
  of paper and board, 49
  materials for, 62
  of paste, 31
  preventing acid migration dur-
    ing, 82
Straight edge, 28, 29, 45
  in cutting mending strips, 70
  in making cradles for book dis-
    play, 182
  in spine repair, 147
  in tipping-in, 94, 96
Strathmore 400, 54
String and twine
  see also Cord
  in making wraparounds, 167, 168
  Seine twine, 54
Stub, of tip-in, 94-95
  adding transparent stub, 96-97
Super cloth, 54, 130
Suppliers, of book repair materials,
    55-57
  by type of material, 58-59
Supports
  for bookplating, 90
  for displaying books, 178-83
  for display labels, 195
  for handling paper, 82
  materials for, 62
  for mending, 69-70
  wedge-shaped, 180

Table, for drying or flattening, 42

Tape
  double-faced, see Double-faced
    tape
  masking, 52
  pressure-sensitive, mending
    with, 21
Tearing
  mending strips, 71
  paper, to determine grain direc-
    tion, 23
Tears, repairing, 68
  edge tears, 72-73
  in pages of bookblock, 69-70
  overlapping tears, 74-77
  reinforcement, 77-79
Telephone book, as source of waste
    sheets, 54
Temperature
  book deterioration and, 20
  exhibition materials and, 175
Tenjugo, 52
Textblock, 17
Text, of a book, 12
Threads, 54
  waxed, 120
  warp and weft, 26
Tipping-in, 91-103
  equipment and materials for, 92
  large number of leaves (guarding),
    98-100
  measuring for, 93-94
  several folded sheets, 101-2
  several single leaves, 97-98
  single leaf, 94-97
  single folded sheet, 101
  torn or cut-out pages, 103
Transparent stubs, 96-97
Triangle, 45
Twine, see String and twine

Ultrasonic welding, 83
Ultraviolet filters, 45, 175
Usumino, 52
Utility knife, 28, 45

Vermin, treatment of, 21

Warp threads, 26
Waste board, 28, 55
  in tipping-in, 96
Waste materials, 54-55
  paper strips, 55
  sheets, 30
Watercolor brushes, 43
  care of, 33

in pasting edges of a tear, 75
Waxed paper, 30
  in bookplating, 90
  in making pamphlet covers, 118
  in matting documents, 193-94
  in mending edge tears, 73
  in mending overlapping tears,
    74, 76
  in mending tears with no over-
    lap, 77, 79
  in repairing broken hinges, 137,
    138
  in spine repair, 145, 150
  in tipping-in, 95-97, 99-100
Waxed paper strips, 55
Waxed thread, in sewing pam-
    phlets, 120
Webbing, polyester, 45, 65-67
Weft threads, 26
Weighting
  for encapsulating documents, 85,
    86
  in repairing overlapping tears,
    76
  in repairing shaken hinges, 156
  in spine repair, 150
  in tipping-in, 99
  pamphlet covers, 124
Weights, 46-48
Wei t'o spray, 51, 83
Welding, ultrasonic see Ultrasonic
    welding
Wetting, to determine grain direc-
    tion, 24
Wheat paste, 31, 55
Whipstitched binding, 13
Wooden board
  15th century binding made of, 19
  for pressing, 40
Wooden lying press, 39
Workbench
  instructions for building, 34-35
  storage of materials in, 49
Wraparounds, 163-70
  equipment and materials for, 159
  grain direction for, 22
  inner wrapper, 164
  measuring for, 162-63
  outer wrapper, 165-70
  scoring and folding, 160-61
Wrappers, see Kyle wrappers; Wrap-
    arounds

Zigzag stitch, in encapsulation, 88-
    89

Design and illustrations are by Jane Greenfield.

The basic type face for the book is
Smith-Carona Regency Elite. The index
was set in Bembo and the chapter titles in Melior.

Port City Press, Baltimore, MD, printed the
book on 60-pound cream-white acid-free
paper supplied by Miami Paper Mills,
West Carrollton, OH.

Short Run Bindery, Medford, NJ, bound the book
in Buckram cloth supplied by Joanna Western Mills,
Kingsport, TN.

BOOKS -- THEIR CARE AND REPAIR

	DATE DUE		